FACTORY STORE GUIDE TO ALL NEW ENGLAND

The
Pequot
Press

Chester, Connecticut 06412

BY A. MISER & A. PENNYPINCHER

THIRD EDITION

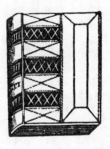

Library of Congress Catalog Card Number: 76-51130
ISBN: 0-87106-076-0
Manufactured in the United States of America

FOREWORD

With this fourth edition of the *Guide To Factory Stores,* the housewife concerned with stretching her budget must continue to look diligently for ways to expand her purchasing power.

Fortunately, the expansion of manufacturing concerns offering their merchandise directly to the public appears to keep pace with that need.

Factory stores usually are not plush, it is this very lack of plushness that helps keep the prices down. If you are shopping for a new dress, do you really need wall-to-wall carpeting, or would you rather be able to purchase the dress at 50% of the normal retail price?

Almost without exception, we have found the stores we visited to be neat and clean, and the sales clerks unusually courteous and helpful.

Merchandise offered may be first quality, overruns, off-season, or irregular. The savings range from 20% to 60%, and will be even greater on special sales items.

In some areas, you will find clusters of stores. Bridgeport, Connecticut, the Industry Yard in Worcester, Massachusetts, New Bedford and Fall River, Massachusetts, and Portsmouth, New Hampshire are a few of the localities where this occurs.

Whenever possible, telephone numbers have been included. Stores do go out of business, change their hours, or close for vacation; a call ahead is a wise precaution.

If saving money is important to you, this Guide can be helpful. Any inconveniences are usually outweighed by the year long benefits. If you accustom yourself to the challenge of stretching your dollars, everything from shoes to hats, from toiletries to rugs, from lingerie to outerwear, from necessities to gifts, can be purchased at a factory store, at substantial savings.

A. Miser
A. Pennypincher

Branford   *Clothing (Men's, Women's)*

MOSTLY MEN OF BRANFORD
280 East Main Street
(Rustic Barn Shoppes)
Tel. #203-488-4194
Monday-Saturday 10:00-5:30
Thursday till 8:30
BankAmericard and Master Charge

Mostly Men features an excellent assortment of men's shirts, ties, and sweaters, and sportswear for women including slacks, shirts, and tops. There is a good selection of sizes, and the choice of shirt styles and colors should yield something for almost every man.

Parking is easy, and the sales personnel helpful.

AMERICAN FABRICS COMPANY
1015 Connecticut Avenue
Tel. #203-335-2151
Monday-Friday 10:00-5:00
Saturday 9:00-12:00

Beautiful fabrics, including lace, eyelet, and brocades, as well as trimmings by the yard, appliques, and some tablecloths are among the items to be found here. The selection is certainly adequate if you are a sewer and are interested in enchantingly feminine yard goods. If you are a crafts person, working on holiday projects, there might also be just the piece of lace or embroidered fabric you need for your craft.

Bridgeport   *Yarns, Blankets*

AMERICAN WOOLEN COMPANY
805 Wood Avenue
Tel. #203-579-1650
Monday-Saturday 9:00-6:00
Wednesday and Thursday till 9:00
BankAmericard and Master Charge

The American Woolen Company offers an
excellent assortment of woolen knitting yarns and a
variety of needlecraft supplies and kits. The
knitting wool can be purchased on mill cones and in
jumbo skeins. In addition, both woolen and
synthetic fiber blankets are available.

Classes in various craft activities have been held;
inquire for more specific information.

Selection and savings make a visit here most
worthwhile.

Bridgeport   *Watches, Jewelry*

BENRUS
215 Warren Street
University Square
Tel. #203-576-0670
Tuesday-Saturday 10:00-5:00
Master Charge

The Benrus store features watches for both men
and women. It has also some very attractive
jewelry, including pins, necklaces, earrings, and
bracelets for women, and a few cuff link sets and tie
tacks for men.

Well worth a visit if you are looking for a watch.

Bridgeport   *Clothing (Men's, Women's)*
                                Shoes (Men's, Women's)

CAROLINA FACTORY OUTLET, INC.
215 Warren Street
Tel. #203-336-2526, 203-336-2527
Monday-Wednesday, Saturday 9:30-6:00
Thursday and Friday 7:30-9:00

The Carolina Factory Outlet is a very large store offering an extensive assortment of items for men and women. Bostonian shoes are featured for men, with socks and underwear also available; for women, one of the most extensive selections of stockings is available, as well as a large selection of handbags, an excellent assortment of scarves, shoes, nightgowns and robes, and knee socks.

The quantity and the excellent selection combine to make this well worth a visit.

Bridgeport   *Paper Goods*

EASTERN BAG AND PAPER COMPANY
459 Iranistan Avenue
Tel. #203-334-4112
Monday-Friday 8:00-4:45
Saturday 9:00-1:00

This outlet store for a major distributor of paper goods offers everything from bags to holiday and party paper goods. The range of merchandise is excellent, and offers the shopper a multitude of items.

Bridgeport   *Giftware*

INTERNATIONAL SILVER FACTORY STORE
215 Warren Street (University Square)
Tel. #203-334-2872
Monday-Wednesday, Saturday 10:00-6:00
Thursday and Friday 10:00-9:00
Master Charge

   See Meriden, Connecticut listing.

Bridgeport   *Clothing (Women's)*

LEVINE COAT CO. OF BRIDGEPORT, INC.
27 Harrison Street
Tel. #203-335-6468
Monday-Saturday 9-5:30
Thursday till 8:30
BankAmericard and Master Charge

Levine's offers an impressive collection of women's clothing.

A wide variety of coats, including dress styles, raincoats, car coats, and spring coats will be found. The choices include suede, cloth, fur trim, and the fake fur. Dresses, blouses, skirts, pant suits, and sportswear are also featured here.

The sales personnel are most helpful, the selection is terrific, off-street parking is available; these factors combined with the excellent savings make this a store well worth a visit!

Bridgeport   *Leather and Suede*
                              Clothing (Men's, Women's)

MAIN MODES, INC.
1225 Connecticut Avenue
Tel. #203-366-3565
Monday-Friday 10:00-3:00
BankAmericard and Master Charge

Now at a new location, Main Modes continues to
carry an excellent selection of genuine leather and
suede coats, jackets, and sportswear. Only leather
and suede are found here; an ample variety of styles
and sizes is available.

Ample parking is available.

Alterations are free and a layaway plan is
available.

There are occasional Sunday sales scheduled, but
check on these by phone before planning a Sunday
visit. Also check before planning a summer visit.

Bridgeport   *Sleepwear (Women's)*

MITCHELL BROTHERS, INC.
345 Railroad Avenue
Tel. #203-334-6105
Saturday only 9:30-4:00

An excellent assortment of sleepwear and loungewear is available at Mitchell Brothers. Nightgowns, pajamas, and robes will be found in an ample selection of fabrics, styles, sizes, and colors. In addition, some lace trims are available.

A visit here should be worthwhile.

Bridgeport   *Shoes (Women's)*

PAPPAGALLO SHOE OUTLET
1693 Park Avenue
Tel. #203-333-3338
Monday-Saturday 10:00-5:30

This small outlet has an ample selection of famous name shoes. There is a broad range of sizes, colors, and styles. A visit here would seem to be worthwhile, as it would be hard not to find one pair of shoes suited to your particular tastes.

Parking is on the street.

Bridgeport   *Clothing (Women's)*

QUALITY COAT FACTORY
40 Cowles Street
Tel. #203-335-8115
Monday-Friday 8:00-4:00
Saturday 8:00-1:00

The Quality Coat Factory store offers all purpose
coats, rainwear, and suits in an excellent range of
styles, sizes, and colors. The choice is certainly
ample, and shopping here is a pleasant experience.

Bridgeport   *Furniture*

TECH FURNITURE FACTORY CLEARANCE
CENTER
450 Hancock Avenue (Cherry & Hancock)
Tel. #203-333-4541
Saturday and Sunday (except holidays) 10:00-4:00
Master Charge

At the Factory Clearance Center will be found an
extensive assortment of contemporary designer
furniture including sofas, love seats, club chairs,
swivel tub chairs, buffets, etageres, and occasional
tables. The prices are at wholesale; if your taste is
for the contemporary design, a visit here will be
very worthwhile.
   The large selection, the easy access, and the
helpful sales personnel are factors which, combined
with the savings, make a trip here worthwhile.

Bridgeport   *Clothing (Men's, Women's,*
Children's)

WARNACO OUTLET STORE
130 Gregory Street
Tel. #203-579-8164
Monday-Saturday 10:00-6:00
Thursday, Friday till 9:00

One of the largest clothing factory stores, the Warnaco Outlet Store offers the products of all the apparel divisions of Warnaco, Inc. A tremendous selection of clothing for men, women, and children is available, with excellent choices of sizes, styles, and colors. Ranging from lingerie for women to jackets for men, the store cannot help but be a tremendous asset to everyone's clothing budget.

This must be ranked as one of the most outstanding of the factory stores.

Centerbrook   *Lighting Fixtures*

COLONIAL BRASS CRAFTSMAN
Essex Industrial Park
Westbrook Road
Tel. #203-767-0769
Monday-Friday 9:00-4:00
Saturday 9:00-5:00

A delightful selection of authentic reproductions of traditional American lighting fixtures will be found here. Oil burning lamps as well as electrical fixtures are available in brass, copper, pewter and tin. Also shades may be purchased separately.

The ample selection and the ease of parking make a shopping trip here a pleasant one.

Colchester   *Clothing (Women's)*

ADLER'S FACTORY OUTLET
Lebanon Avenue
Tel. #203-537-2090
Sunday-Friday 9:00-5:00

Adler's is a delightful outlet in which to shop for coats, pant suits, dress suits, and skirts. There is a nice selection of styles, sizes, and colors available, and the sales personnel are most helpful.

Colchester   *Clothes (Women's, Men's)*

LEVINE AND LEVINE CO., INC.
Lebanon Avenue
Tel. #203-537-2373
Sunday-Friday 9:00-4:30

   Levine and Levine offers an excellent selection of
coats and sportswear. Harris tweeds in numerous
shades are featured, with raincoats, all-weather
coats, pant suits, and sportswear to be found in a
wide range of styles, sizes, and colors. A recent
addition are coats for men; a good choice is available
in the men's department.
   The sales personnel are helpful without being
overwhelming, the selection is ample, the parking is
adequate; these factors combine to make a shopping
trip here a pleasant experience.

Danbury   *Hats & Headwear (Men's)*

DANBURY HAT CO.,
FACTORY STORE OUTLET
89 Rose Hill Avenue
Tel. #203-743-2715
Friday and Saturday 9:30-5:00

For the man who wants chic-appeal (sans serif) at attractive prices, this is the place to come. Worth an historic visit for this is the home of the famous "Stetson".

Danbury   *Clothing (Women's, Men's)*

GRAND FASHION OUTLET
48 Shalvay Lane
Tel. #203-743-4603
Tuesday, Wednesday, Friday 11:00-5:00

This store features an attractive assortment of women's clothing, including suits, long skirts, slacks, shorts, culottes, pant suits, dresses, sweaters, and robes. The choice of sizes, styles, and colors should be adequate for most shoppers.

Men's items include sweaters and sport pants.

If your clothing budget needs some help, this is a good place to visit.

SEWER'S DELIGHT
Roosevelt Drive
Tel. #203-735-1600
Tuesday, Wednesday, Friday, Saturday 9:00-5:00
Monday and Thursday 10:00-9:00

If you are a sewer, this is well worth a visit. A
large selection of knit fabrics is to be found here,
with the choice of color and pattern offering
something for almost every possible need. It seems
as if most visitors end up picking out "just one
more" of the pre-cut lengths.

TIFFANY HOUSE
304 Seymour Avenue
Tel. #203-735-2050
Sunday-Friday 10:30-5:00
BankAmericard and Master Charge

This factory outlet store features an extensive line of Tiffany style lighting fixtures. Both hanging and flush-to-the-ceiling styles are available in a wide selection of handcrafted stained glass patterns. The typical flower shapes and the muted colors traditionally associated with the Tiffany style are available.

If you are looking for an affordable Tiffany style fixture, a trip here will be very worthwhile.

East Hampton   *Toiletries*

HOUSE OF HAMPTON PERFUMES
31 East High Street
Tel. #203-267-4444
Monday-Saturday 9:00-5:00
Sunday 1:00-6:00

This delightful store offers an impressive
selection of toiletry items, including witch hazel and
perfumes. Many of the items are available in
attractive gift containers. Naturally, you may try
the various scents before making a decision.
This store is a most enjoyable one to visit,
offering an excellent choice for most shoppers.

Essex   *Furniture*

THE HITCHCOCK CHAIR STORE
Hitchcock Chair Company
Route 153
Tel. #203-767-8128

See Riverton, Connecticut listing.

SAXONY COAT COMPANY
1443 Dixwell Avenue
Tel. #203-288-3600
Monday-Saturday 10:00-5:30
Thursday till 9:00
Master Charge

The Saxony Coat store maintains an extensive selection of women's coats in an excellent spread of sizes, colors, and styles. There are sport coats, pant coats, and all-weather coats in addition to the anticipated styles.

Saxony does close its store for the summer, normally from early June through the end of July; hence it would be safer to call first before planning a visit during the summer months.

TUDOR HOUSE
929 Sherman Avenue
Tel. #203-288-8451
Occasional only on Saturday and Sunday 9:00-5:00

Although Tudor House only is open occasionally, the quality of the furniture available and the savings should make a phone call to elicit the sales dates worthwhile.

A variety of chairs, sectionals, couches, and sofa beds in an excellent assortment of fabrics will be found. Styles include traditional, contemporary, and early American. It would be difficult to not find a piece of furniture to suit almost every taste or need.

Hartford *Coats (Leather)*

SNYDER LEATHER FACTORY OUTLET
225 Brainard Road
Tel. #203-247-2933
Monday-Wednesday 10:00-6:00
Thursday and Friday 10:00-9:00
Saturday 9:00-5:00
BankAmericard and Master Charge

See Brighton, Massachusetts listing.

Jewett City   *Fabrics (Curtain & Drape)*

FABRICS 84
Route 12 (Exit 84 off Route 52)
Tel. #203-376-4441
Monday-Saturday 9:00-5:00

An excellent assortment of curtain and drapery fabrics will be found here. If you are moving into a new home or are currently remodeling, and are a sewer, this would be a good choice for selecting fabrics. Be sure to bring the measurements of your windows; charts are posted for computing yardage, and the clerks are extremely helpful, but without your window measurements, no one can help.

BEZZINI'S OLD COLONY COMPANY
Adams and Hilliard Streets
Tel. #203-649-3183
Open once a year (twice in 1976)
Master Charge, lay-a-way, extended payment plans

The assortment of furniture offered in the once a year sale is unbelievable. The savings make it well worth the phone call to elicit the date for the coming year! Sofas, love seats, sleep sofas, chairs, and ottomans are offered in a tremendous range of styles and fabrics. It would be difficult to imagine that a visit here would not be worthwhile.

On the sale day, you can order custom made furniture; the opportunity to buy at direct factory prices extends to this category, also.

CONNECTICUT GIFT SHOP
Div. of Silver City Glass Co., Inc.
71 Parker Avenue
Tel. #203-237-0429
Monday-Saturday 9:30-5:30

Featured here are lovely sterling silver on glass items, ranging from cake plates to decorative bowls to vases. These pieces make lovely gifts and are certainly most attractive for wedding or anniversaries. Other gift items are also available here.

The store is delightful, and certainly offers a temptation to purchase for oneself as well as for gifts!

CONN. HOUSE PEWTERERS
443 South Colony Street
Tel. #203-634-0555
Monday-Friday 9:00-4:00
Tuesday-Friday Evenings 6:30-9:30
Saturday 9:00-3:00

A nice assortment of pewter candlesticks, Revere style bowls, trays, goblets, candy dishes, and chargers will be found here. The pewter is handcrafted, an operation fascinating in itself.

If you are partial to pewter, a trip here is particularly enjoyable.

INTERNATIONAL SILVER FACTORY STORE
500 South Broad Street
Tel. #203-634-2000
Monday-Friday 9:30-5:30
Saturday 9:30-4:00
Master Charge

BRANCH STORE:
215 Warren Street (University Square)
Tel. #203-334-2872
Monday-Wednesday, Saturday 10:00-6:00
Thursday and Friday 10:00-9:00
Master Charge

The International Silver Factory Store offers an impressive assortment of silver, pewter and gold electroplated items. Everything from punch bowls to serving trays to candle holders to napkin rings can be found here. Gift items such as pewter figures and Christmas items such as special ornaments will also be found.

In addition to the wide selection, the sales personnel are most helpful. A trip to this delightful store is both enjoyable and financially helpful to the budget.

THE ROCKWELL SILVER COMPANY
24 Randolph Avenue
Tel. #203-238-7800
Monday-Friday 9:00-4:45
Saturday 9:00-12:00 (Check as this varies)

A beautiful selection of sterling silver on glassware will be found here. All Rockwell items of sterling silver are offered with a special non-tarnish finish. A choice of several flower patterns as well as monograms and anniversary patterns is available with items including vases, cake plates, trays, compotes, and candlesticks.

Delightful to visit, and most helpful to the gift segment of the family budget!

Naugatuck   *Mattresses*

THE BEDDING FACTORY OUTLET
26 Hotchkiss Street
Tel. #203-729-6437
Monday-Saturday 9:00-6:00

This outlet offers mattresses and box springs in twin, full, queen, and king sizes. Delivery, within a reasonable distance, can be arranged.

KENSINGTON FACTORY STORE
102 Washington Street
Tel. #203-225-6389
Sunday only 10:00-5:00
Master Charge

The Kensington Factory Store offers an excellent line of designer sportswear including slacks, shirts, skirts, pant suits, blazers, sweaters, leather jackets, pant coats, and coats. Sizes, styles, and colors are offered in an excellent selection.

Also to be found are fabric, buttons, zippers, and seam binding.

Ample parking is available.

The store is closed from mid June through the summer, so a check by phone is wise, before making a trip here.

New Hartford   *Furniture*

TOWNSHEND FURNITURE CO., INC.
Route 44
Tel. #203-379-4341
Tuesday-Saturday 10:00-5:00
Sunday 12:00-5:00
Master Charge

See Townshend, Vermont listing.

New Hartford   *Small Appliances*

WARING PRODUCTS
FACTORY OUTLET STORE
Route 44
Tel. #203-379-0731
Monday-Friday 9:00-3:00

An excellent assortment of the Waring appliances
is available at the Outlet Store. Blenders, blender
accessories, hand mixers, stand mixers, can
openers, juicers, and ice crushers are to be found in
all the Waring colors and styles. Special close out
items are featured from time to time.

The availability of service on the Waring
appliances, the range of choices, the parking
facilities, and the helpful sales personnel are all
factors which make a trip here most worthwhile.

New Haven   *Lingerie, Clothing (Women's,*
                                          Children's)

BERGER FACTORY OUTLET
135 Derby Avenue
Tel. #203-624-0131
Wednesday-Saturday 9:30-4:00
Thursday till 6:00
BankAmericard and Master Charge

The Berger Factory Outlet offers an excellent
assortment of girdles, bras, and lingerie, as well as
some sportswear for women.

The newly added girl's department offers dresses,
tops, skirts, and slacks in sizes 3-6X and 7-14.

The ample selection and the helpful sales
personnel are factors which, combined with the
savings, make a shopping trip here worthwhile.

New Haven   *Clothing (Men's, Women's)*

GANT OUTLET STORE
40 Sargent Drive
Tel. #203-772-2450
Monday-Friday 9:00-4:30
Saturday 9:00-4:00
Courtesy Pass may be required

This outlet features Gant shirts for men, and offers an excellent assortment of sizes and colors. In addition, a wide selection of sweaters, ties, belts, sport clothes for men, and blouses, skirts, and sport clothes for women is also to be found.

Since the store is directly accessible from Route 95, a trip here is easily accomplished.

New Haven   *Fabrics*

KAHAN WOOL GRADING CORP.
71 Prince Street
Tel. #203-865-8208
Monday-Friday 9:00-5:30
Saturday 10:00-4:00

An excellent selection of fabrics will be found here, ranging from woolens for coats and suits to drapery sheers. The assortment varies with the season, but seems always sure to yield bargains for the home sewer.

The excellent savings make a trip here worthwhile.

New Haven   *Clothing (Women's)*

MAY COAT COMPANY
430 Congress Avenue
Tel. #203-776-2759
Sunday-Friday 9:00-5:00
Closed early June to early September

An outstanding assortment of women's wear will be found at the factory outlet of the May Coat Company. Coats in an excellent range of styles and fabrics, pants, skirts, blazers, separates, tops, and sweaters in both junior and misses sizes are all available. The range of choices is really very large.

There is an off-street parking lot where one hour of free parking is given when you make a purchase.

Well worth a visit.

ONLY SHIRTS
550 Whalley Avenue
Tel. #203-389-2513
Monday-Saturday 10:00-5:30
Closes during July and August

Only Shirts offers just what its name says — an extensive assortment of several famous makers lines of men's shirts. Long and short sleeve styles in dress, sport, leisure, and golf shirts are available in an excellent range of styles and colors. In addition, big and tall man sizes are available.

If you are restocking in the shirt department, a trip here should prove worthwhile.

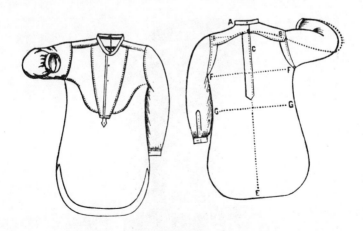

SLEEP STUFF, Inc.
11 East Pearl Street
Tel. #203-624-2186
Monday-Friday 9:30-4:00

At this outlet store, an excellent selection of women's robes, pajamas, long and short nightgowns, aprons, smocks, dusters, beach robes, slacks, blouses, shorts, pant suits, and tank tops is available. Found in sizes of 10-18, 38-44, and XL-XXL, there should be something for everyone. The choices of colors and styles are good.

A visit here should be most helpful to the clothing budget.

TONI'S FACTORY STORE
433 Chapel Street
Tel. #203-562-2145
Daily 10:00-5:00
Sundays during May, June and July

The Toni Factory Store offers a good assortment of swimsuits for ladies. Both one and two piece styles are available of several famous brands. An intriguing feature is the mix 'n' match; in the two piece suits, you can purchase a top of one size and a bottom of another. Since few of us have those perfect, true to size figures, this is a wonderful way to compensate for the imperfections.

In addition, some items such as zippers, thread, fabric, and sewing notions are available.

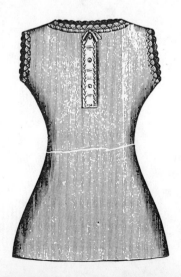

FACTORY OUTLET
92 Garfield Avenue
Tel. #203-443-1843
Monday-Friday 11:00-4:00
Sunday 11:00-4:00

A good selection of winter outerwear, all-weather coats, and windbreakers for all members of the family will be found here. The choice of sizes and colors is adequate; if you are looking to save on the winter clothing budget, a stop here may be helpful.

In addition, fabrics are also available.

New London   *Clothing (Men's, Boy's)*

THE FACTORY STORE
Hendel Manufacturing Company
75 Crystal Avenue
Tel. #203-443-4353
Monday-Friday 9:00-4:00
Saturday 9:00-12:00

An excellent assortment of clothing for men and boys is offered here. Jackets, sport shirts, bathing suits, shorts, sweaters, sweat shirts, windbreakers, and underwear are found in a wide range of sizes and colors. The items are excess stock and overruns.

In addition to the desirable savings here, if you drive to the end of the street, the railroad turntable of the Central Vermont Railroad may be seen.

North Grosvenordale   *Clothing (Men's)*

QUINN'S SHIRT SHOP
Route 12
Tel. #203-923-2981
Monday-Saturday 10:00-4:00

An excellent assortment of shirts for men will be found here. Also available are pajamas, underwear, sweaters, ties, and socks.

A broad range of styles, sizes, and colors is available.

Helpful place to shop; any clothing budget should profit from a shopping trip here.

GILTEX
14 Middletown Avenue
Tel. #203-288-8411
Sunday-Friday 9:00-9:00

Giltex offers a tremendous range of merchandise of the kind normally found in chain stores and supermarkets. Clothing such as underwear, socks, shirts, tops, and lingerie, sneakers, boots, household items such as tablecloths, scatter rugs, and sundries are among the hundreds of items available.

The extensive array, easy parking, and ample shopping hours are features which, combined with the savings offered, make this a logical place to shop.

DECKER'S
692 West Avenue
Tel. #203-866-5593
Monday-Saturday 9:30-5:30
Wednesday till 8:00

BRANCH STORE:
334 Windsor Avenue
Windsor
Tel. #203-728-6733
Monday-Saturday 9:30-5:30
Wednesday till 9:30

Decker's offers an excellent stock of clothing, including shirts, sweaters, belts, and ties. A wide range of styles, colors, and sizes is always available. It would seem that any visit here would be a successful one, for the quality, the selection, and the savings should please almost everyone.

INTIMATE APPAREL FACTORY OUTLET
618 Main Avenue (Route #7)
Tel. #203-846-2488
Monday-Saturday 9:30-5:30
Thursday and Friday till 9:00

This is an excellent store offering a well-known manufacturer's line of lingerie, bras, and girdles. Women's sweaters will also be found.

Samples, overruns, and seconds are all available; the choice of styles and sizes is ample.

Your lingerie budget will benefit from a shopping trip here.

Norwich   *Footwear (Men's, Boy's)*

CENTRAL SHOE MFG. CO., INC.
5 Wisconsin Avenue
(Norwich Industrial Park)
Tel. #203-886-1401
Monday-Friday 9:00-4:00
Saturday 9:00-12:00

Shoes for the male members of the family will be
found here, with styles including oxfords, loafers,
boots, hi-cuts, and slippers. The choice is excellent
with ample stock available to meet size and style
choices.

Norwich   *Clothing (Women's)*

THE MAPLE TREE
35 Chestnut Street
Tel. #203-887-8110
Monday-Friday 9:00-9:00
Saturday 9:00-5:00
Sunday 10:00-4:00

See Old Saybrook, Connecticut listing.

KAREN MILL OUTLET
Route 97
Tel. #203-822-8238
Monday-Saturday 9:30-4:00

This store offers an excellent assortment of
screen-printed drapery and curtain fabrics. The
colors and designs should yield something to meet
your needs.

Be sure to bring window measurements along, for
no one can help you determine the yardage you need,
unless you have those measurements with which to
work.

Old Lyme   *Wooden Accessories*
                                  for Needlework

FACTORY SHOP of SUDBERRY HOUSE
Colton Road
Tel. #203-739-6951
Monday-Friday 9:00-4:00
Saturday 9:00-1:00

This is a delightful shop, containing Sudberry's fine line of wooden accessories for needlework, and including a specially designed group of kits to fit their wooden items. Footstools, a beautiful child-size Queen Anne chair, trays, game boards, etc. are available; what beautiful heirloom gifts a creative needleworker can make.

The atmosphere is distinctly friendly and helpful, and the selection is excellent, making a trip here a pleasant experience.

THE MAPLE TREE
Old Saybrook Shopping Center
Route 1
Tel. #203-388-0344
Monday-Saturday 10:00-5:30
Thursday till 9:00

BRANCH STORE:
35 Chestnut Street
Norwich
Tel. #203-887-8110
Monday-Friday 9:00-9:00
Saturday 9:00-5:00
Sunday 10:00-4:00

The Maple Tree features "famous maker women's wear" from a Connecticut manufacturer. Labels advertised recently have included Pierre Cardin, Bonjour, Maverick, and Landlubber. Jackets, skirts, jumpsuits, knit tops, tennis dresses, slacks, tops, dresses, long skirts, and pant suits are available.

WELLINGTON CURTAIN FACTORY STORE
83 Canal Street
Tel. #203-928-7475
Monday-Friday 9:30-5:00
Saturday 9:00-1:00

The Wellington Store offers an outstanding selection of curtains, draperies, bedspreads, and related household accessories. The choice of sizes, styles, and colors is certainly ample.

The selection, the helpful sales personnel, and the adequate parking are all factors combining to make this a worthwhile shopping place.

THE HITCHCOCK CHAIR STORE
Hitchcock Chair Company
Route 20
Tel. #203-379-4826
Monday-Saturday 9:00-5:00
BankAmericard and Master Charge

BRANCH STORES:
Route 153
Essex, Connecticut
Tel. #203-767-8128

Route 7
Wilton, Connecticut
Tel. #203-762-9594

The entire Hitchcock line of furniture is available at their stores. The furniture is authentically reproduced; the factory has currently been in operation since 1946 and the furniture pieces presently being made are true copies of the original Hitchcock furniture.

An interesting museum is located in Riverton making a trip to the parent location particularly interesting.

SHELTON HOSIERY MILLS, INC.
549 Howe Avenue
Tel. #203-735-4686
Thursday and Friday 10:00-4:00
Saturday 10:00-1:00

An excellent selection of hosiery for men, women,
and children will be found here. Knee socks, dress
socks, gym socks, stockings, and support hose are
available in a good range of sizes and colors.

Stamford   *Clothes (Women's)*

LADY CARLTON COAT CO., INC.
63 Stillwater Avenue
Tel. #203-325-2233
Monday-Saturday 9:30-5:30
Master Charge, BankAmericard

A quick note: when you reach the parking lot look
for a sign that reads, "Carlton Deb Factory
Salesroom," and there you will find a wide variety of
women's cloth coats, jackets in wool and all weather
fabrics, synthetic furs, and all seasonal fabrics from
6 to 24½. This store features medium and better
priced sportswear, pants, blouses, sweaters, and
jackets. Of course, the season determines what will
be on the racks at a given time.

DESIGNER'S FACTORY OUTLET
1616 Barnum Avenue
Tel. #203-377-4559
Thursday 10:00-9:00
Friday, Saturday, Sunday 10:00-5:00

There is no doubt but that this store offers one of the most extensive selections of well known names in the fashion world. Not one, but several, famous names in the ready-to-wear labels will be found at varying savings. The clothes are neatly hung and carefully protected, the store is attractively maintained, and the selection of sizes and colors should make almost any shopping trip here a successful one.

Thomaston   *Clocks, Watches*

SETH THOMAS YANKEE CLOCK SHOP
South Main Street
Tel. #203-283-5881
Tuesday-Friday 10:00-5:00
Saturday 10:00-3:00
Extended hours prior to Christmas
Master Charge

This is a delightful shop, with an extensive
assortment of clocks and watches available. Both
striking and chiming clocks are available as well as
those which are eminently silent, but all of which
tell time most accurately. Electric, battery, and key
wind models are available in grandfather, mantel,
wall, and desk clocks. A variety of alarm clocks will
be found, as well as a fine selection of watches.

This is certainly one of the most enjoyable stores
to visit, and well worth a trip!

THE PANTS POCKET
Majestic Trouser Co. Factory Outlet
Route 32 (Between Norwich & New London)
Tel. #203-848-1445
Thursday and Friday 10:00-8:00
Saturday and Sunday 10:00-5:00

Sportswear for both men and women in the latest styles and colors is available here. A good selection of sizes in slacks, sportscoats, shirts, belts, blouses and like items will be found.

CHAS. W. HOUSE & SONS, INC.
FACTORY STORE
19 Perry Street
Monday through Saturday 9:30-4:30

A large selection of cascade woolen fabrics at good factory store prices, over 200 styles and colors. Solids, plaids, tweeds, and coordinates and tartans for sportswear and outerwear. Their selections cover wool blends and polyester fabrics, blankets wool and wool blend, billiard cloth, decorative pressed felts, and woolens for rug making, braiding and hooking. Great spot for the person who likes to sew.

Wauregan   *Fabrics, Clothing*
                              (Men's, Women's)

WAUREGAN MILLS
Routes 12 and 205
Tel. #203-774-8491
Monday-Thursday 10:00-9:00
Friday 10:00-6:00
Sunday 11:00-6:00

Master Charge and BankAmericard

Wauregan Mills is a delightful store to visit, for a great variety of shopping can be accomplished in one stop! An excellent assortment of fabrics and related sewing items is available, as well as an ample selection of men's shirts, sweaters, socks, ties, and underwear, and women's sportswear including skirts, tops, turtleneck shirts, and blouses. The range of styles, sizes, and colors should yield something for almost every shopper.

MADEWELL OUTLET
74 Clark Street
Tel. #203-932-4093
Monday-Saturday 10:00-5:00
Master Charge

The Madewell Outlet carries a nice variety of sportswear in sizes 8-18. Available are their ladies shirts, long skirts, short skirts, pants, halters, and shells. Their items are part of the daily factory production, so you are almost always assured of a good choice of sizes, styles, and colors.

Westport *Game Tables*

BRUNSWICK LEISURE MART
Brunswick Corp.
877 Post Road, East
Tel. #203-226-6166
Monday-Friday 10:00-9:00
Saturday 10:00-6:00
BankAmericard and Master Charge

The Leisure Mart offers several models of pool tables, hockey game tables, court handball game tables, table tennis, home pinball machines, and multi purpose game tables. In addition, a variety of accessories such as cues, balls, racks, billiard lamps, and other items are available.

If you are furnishing a family game room, a trip here should be most helpful.

Westport   *Clothing (Men's)*

NATIONAL BRANDS STORE
877 Post Road East
Tel. #203-227-8408
Monday-Saturday 10:00-10:00
BankAmericard and Master Charge

The motto of the National Brands Store is to "dress smart without buying dumb." The store offers an assortment of nationally known designers and manufacturers, carrying suits, sport coats, slacks, leather jackets, and outerwear. The selection is quite ample, with a wide range of choices in styles, colors, and sizes.

Certainly worth a visit if you are hopeful of making a dent in the clothing budget.

Wethersfield   *Giftware*

SHERWOOD FACTORY GIFT STORE
1805 Berlin Turnpike
Tel. #203-563-2659
Monday-Friday 11:00-7:00
Saturday and Sunday 11:00-5:00

See Westfield, Massachusetts listing.

Wilton   *Furniture*

THE HITCHCOCK CHAIR STORE
Hitchcock Chair Company
Route #7
Tel. #203-762-9594

See Riverton, Connecticut listing.

Windsor   *Clothing (Men's)*

DECKER'S
334 Windsor Avenue
Tel. #203-728-6733
Monday-Saturday 9:30-5:30
Wednesday till 9:30

See Norwalk, Connecticut listing.

GAMECRAFT FACTORY
30 Hazel Terrace
Tel. #203-397-0233
Daily 9:00-4:00

Gamecraft offers a variety of game tables, including slate pool tables, air hockey, ping pong, and bumper pool tables. Equipment for pool, weight sets, and weight benches are also available here.

If you are interested, you can also watch the tables being made.

INTERNATIONAL KNITTING MILL OUTLET STORE
500 Main Street (Hartford Turnpike)
Tel. #203-269-4148
Monday-Friday 1:00-6:00
Sunday 10:00-3:00

An excellent assortment of sweaters is available at the International Outlet Store. The sweaters offered in this outlet are knitted in the mill. The choice of colors and sizes is excellent, and the adequate parking, helpful sales personnel, and financial savings all combine to make this a store worth visiting.

Bristol   *Footwear*

CONVERSE RUBBER COMPANY
Buttonwood Street
Tel. #401-253-6201
Monday-Saturday 8:30-5:00

See Malden, Massachusetts listing.

Cranston   *Jewelry*

SAMMARTINO DIAMONDS
1468 Elmwood Avenue (Rte. 1A)
Tel. #401-781-0519
Monday-Thursday 9:00-9:00
Friday 9:00-6:00

This beautiful store carries an excellent
assortment of quality jewelry, including 12 karat
gold rings, earrings, pins, and pendants, set with
diamonds, sapphires, rubies, emeralds, opals, etc. In
addition, it handles special orders, remounting, and
repair work.

EAST PROVIDENCE CLOTHING
FACTORY MILL OUTLET
360 Taunton Avenue
Tel. #401-438-3974
Monday-Friday 10:00-9:00
Saturday 10:00-5:30
BankAmericard and Master Charge

BRANCH STORE:
Pontiac Mills Factory Outlet
334 Knight Street (off Rte. 5)
Warwick, Rhode Island
Tel. #401-738-5282
Monday-Friday 10:00-9:00
Saturday 10:00-6:00
BankAmericard and Master Charge

An excellent selection of men's sport coats, suits, slacks, and shirts is to be found at this Mill Outlet. The choice of styles, sizes, and colors is ample, and should provide adequately for almost every taste.

In addition to the clothing, yard goods are also available here.

A trip here should be most helpful to the clothing budget.

Greenville   *Clothing (Men's)*

RONEL STORE
475 Putnam Pike
Tel. #401-949-0150

The Ronel Store offers a nice selection of men's clothing including sportswear and jeans. Also available are yarns and fabrics.

Hamilton (North Kingston)   *Sewing Trimmings*

HAMILTON WEBB CO.
Route #1A
Tel. #401-294-9531
Saturday morning only

Each Saturday morning, customers are able to buy pre-bagged lots of assorted trimmings, etc. The bags contain intriguing selections and are always worth the price, particularly if you are adventurous about such things!

The procedure only goes on as long as the bagged supply lasts, so it is advisable to arrive at around 9:00.

Lots of fun!

Hope Valley   *Handprinted Linen Towels,*
                                 Calendars, Pictures for
                                              Framing

KAY DEE COUNTRY STORE AND GIFTS
Skunk Hill Road
Tel. #401-539-2100
Monday-Saturday 9:00-5:00
Sunday 1:00-6:00
BankAmericard and Master Charge

Kay Dee certainly is one of the most extensive
and attractive gift stores! Everything you could
possibly want is probably to be found here.

However, the attraction for bargain hunters is its
department featuring the discontinued and/or
slightly irregular hand printed linen towels,
calendars, and ready-to-frame pictures.

Factory tours are scheduled for Monday-Friday
at 9:00-11:00, and 1:00-3:00. Visitors can view the
silk screen printing of the towels and calendars.

MILL OUTLET STORE
Colonial Braided Rug Company
560 Mineral Spring Avenue (Route 15)
Tel. #401-724-6279
Monday-Saturday 10:00-5:00

This continues to be a delightful store, where
customers are genuinely welcomed.

The braided rugs are available in an excellent
range of sizes and colors; it is also possible to order
one to suit your particular color scheme. You may
also order runners or stair treads; all items can be
shipped for you.

If you are looking for a braided rug, a visit here
should be worthwhile.

Pawtucket   *Sweaters (Men's, Women's)*

SWEATER WAREHOUSE
212 Dartmouth Street
Tel. #401-725-5770
Monday-Wednesday 9:00-3:00
Thursday and Friday 9:00-9:00
Saturday 9:00-5:00
BankAmericard and Master Charge

An outstanding assortment of sweaters for men and women will be found at this wholesale outlet. The selection of styles, colors, and sizes should provide something for everyone.

The selection, the helpful sales personnel, and the accessibility from Route 95 combine to make this a worthwhile shopping trip.

Providence   *Clothing (Women's)*

BARGAIN HUNTERS
650 Branch Avenue
Tel. #401-721-2207
Monday-Saturday 10:00-5:00
Thursday and Friday till 9:00

See Clover Bay Retail Outlet, New Bedford, Massachusetts listing.

Providence   *Bedspreads*

BEDSPREAD MILL OUTLET
133 Mathewson Street
Tel. #401-861-9536

   See New Bedford, Massachusetts listing.

Providence   *Coats (Leather)*

SNYDER LEATHER FACTORY OUTLET
708 Elmwood Avenue
Tel. #401-467-4230
Monday-Friday 10:00-9:00
Saturday 9:00-5:00
BankAmericard and Master Charge

   See Brighton, Massachusetts listing.

Warwick   *Clothing (Men's)*

PONTIAC MILLS FACTORY OUTLET
334 Knight Street (Off Rte. 3)
Tel. #401-738-5282
Monday-Friday 10:00-9:00
Saturday 10:00-6:00
BankAmericard and Master Charge

See East Providence Clothing Factory Mill
Outlet, East Providence, Rhode Island listing.

Woonsocket   *Clothing (Men's)*

NEEDLE CRAFT FACTORY OUTLET
565 North Main Street
Tel. #401-766-1000
Monday-Saturday 9:00-5:00
Thursday and Friday till 9:00

An excellent assortment of outdoor jackets for
men and boys will be found at the Needle Craft
Outlet. Available in unlined, light lined, or heavy
lined styles, the range of sizes is certainly ample.
The season for which the factory is currently
producing jackets determines the variety available.

STITCHERS INC.
Retail Remnant Room
1081 Social Street
Tel. #401-767-1500
Monday-Friday 8:00-5:00
Saturday 8:00-12:00

A wide range of fabrics is available here, in remnant lengths and by the pound. Both the home sewer, and the craft oriented person will find the excellent selection to be most helpful. Assorted trims are also available here.

Adams   *Wallpaper, Fabrics*

OLD STONE MILL
Route 8
Tel. #413-743-1015
Monday-Friday 8:30-4:30

If you are redecorating, the Old Stone Mill is the place to start your shopping! The selection of wallpaper is almost unbelievable, with savings which cannot fail to help your redecorating budget. Both colonial and contemporary designs in wallpaper are to be found, and many have matching fabrics available.

Everyone is most helpful, and a trip here is a relaxing, rewarding experience.

Adams   *Clothing (Coats)*

THAT COAT PLACE IN ADAMS
Berkshire Textile Corporation
Commercial Street
Tel. #413-743-0882
Monday-Saturday 9:30-5:30
Thursday and Friday till 9:00
Master Charge

One of the outstanding selections of coats will be
found here. A wide range of styles, sizes, and colors
is available, and rainwear is included in the
selection. Some pant suits are also available.

If you are coat shopping, a trip here should prove
worthwhile.

Amherst   *Clothing (Men's, Women's,*
Children's)

CHARLESTOWN MILL STORE
East Pleasant Street
Tel. #413-549-6670

See Charlestown, New Hampshire listing.

Andover   *Footwear*

CONVERSE RUBBER COMPANY
Route 28
Tel. #617-475-5300
Monday-Saturday 8:30-5:00

See Malden, Massachusetts listing.

Athol   *Shoes (Family)*

THOM McAN FACTORY OUTLET
Lord Pond Plaza
Tel. #617-249-3395
Monday-Saturday 10:00-5:00
Thursday till 9:00
Closed Wednesday

See Dover, New Hampshire listing.

Baldwinville   *Furniture*

DAN'S PINE SHOP FACTORY SHOWROOM
Route #202
Tel. #617-939-5687
Sunday-Saturday 10:00-5:00

Pine furniture, including occasional tables, coffee tables, cribbage tables, small storage units, and a very attractive rocking horse are among the items available here. Both the dark and the honey tone finish are available, and many pieces have hand painted flower designs added.

SNYDER LEATHER FACTORY OUTLET
342 Western Avenue
Tel. #617-782-3300
Monday-Friday 9:00-9:00
Saturday 9:00-5:00
BankAmericard and Master Charge

BRANCH STORES:
Railroad Square
Haverhill, Massachusetts
Tel. #617-372-3381
Monday-Saturday 9:00-5:00
Tuesday and Friday till 9:00
BankAmericard and Master Charge

708 Elmwood Avenue
Providence, Rhode Island
Tel. #401-467-4230
Monday-Friday 10:00-9:00
Saturday 9:00-5:00
BankAmericard and Master Charge

225 Brainard Road
Hartford, Connecticut
Tel. #203-247-2933
Monday-Wednesday 10:00-6:00
Thursday and Friday 10:00-9:00
Saturday 9:00-5:00
BankAmericard and Master Charge

An excellent assortment of leather coats and
jackets for both men and women will be found here.
Sizes for men range from 34-46, and for women from
6-18, with some half sizes available.

Brookline   *China, Glass, Cookware*

CHINA FAIR WAREHOUSE
1638 Beacon Street
Tel. #617-566-2220
Monday-Saturday 9:30-5:00

See Cambridge, Massachusetts listing.

Cambridge   *China, Glass, Cookware*

CHINA FAIR WAREHOUSE
2100 Massachusetts Avenue
Tel. #617-864-3050
Monday-Saturday 10:00-6:00

BRANCH STORES:
1638 Beacon Street
Brookline, Massachusetts
Tel. #617-566-2220
Monday-Saturday 9:30-5:00

70 Needham Street
Newton, Massachusetts
Tel. #617-332-1520
Monday-Saturday 9:00-5:00

This outlet store features imported contemporary glass, dinnerware, and cookware in one of the largest assortments to be found! Over 3,000 items are stocked here, including such things as French vegetable steamers, Lauffer's cast iron cookware, Arabia China, Copco tea kettles, and so on.

The variety is unbelievable and the savings are excellent, making this well worth a visit.

Dartmouth   *Clothing (Women's)*

KAY WINDSOR OUTLET
375 Faunce Corner Road
Tel. #617-998-3311
Monday-Friday 10:00-9:00
Saturday 10:00-5:30

Any woman who enjoys Kay Windsor clothing
will find a visit to this store to be quite a treat!

The store is in a new, modern, attractive facility
with extensive merchandise on the racks. Dresses,
suits, slacks, pant suits, and sportswear will be
found in an excellent assortment of styles, sizes,
and colors.

This store has everything to recommend it; easy
to find, ample parking, extensive selection,
courteous sales people, and many dressing rooms
are all factors which combine with the half price
factor of a well known popular brand to make it an
outstanding factory store.

Douglas   *Fabrics*

THE MILL YARD, INC. OF
Hayward Schuster Mill
Route 16
Tel. #617-476-7411
Tuesday, Thursday, Saturday 10:00-4:00

A nice selection of woolen fabrics will be found
here, available both as remnants and by the yard. If
you are a sewer, or a rug braider, a trip here should
be rewarding. The colors and patterns are tempting.

BROOKFIELD FACTORY OUTLET
Route #9
Tel. #617-867-7406
Monday-Friday 10:00-6:00
Thursday, Friday till 9:00
Saturday 10:00-5:30

The Brookfield Outlet is of special interest to the sports oriented family as it is the home of the Bobby Orr equipment and skates, as well as offering an excellent assortment of athletic footwear and equipment. In addition, it is a shoe outlet offering a good variety of famous name brand shoes for the family, and is most helpful to the shoe and sports budget.

LESNOW OUTLET STORE
Lesnow Manufacturing Company
148 Pleasant Street
Tel. #413-527-0012
Monday-Friday 11:00-9:00
Sunday 10:00-7:00
BankAmericard and Master Charge

An excellent assortment of men's clothing will be
found at the Lesnow Outlet Store. Slacks,
sportcoats, suits, all weather coats, and sport suits
are available in a wide range of sizes, colors, fabrics,
and styling.

With the large selection, the very helpful sales
personnel, and adequate parking, a trip here is both
pleasant and a successful way to save on the
clothing budget.

Fall River   *Jewelry, Giftware*

ANNEX MILL OUTLET
135 Alden Street
Tel. #617-676-0229
Monday-Saturday 10:00-4:00

The Annex Outlet offers "handcrafted wampum and scrimshaw at factory-to-you prices." A unique shop, especially for a factory store guide, but a very special and worth-a-visit-spot for those of you who appreciate the beautiful things of scrimshaw. The crafts involved are painstaking, indeed, but the finished products should well become heirlooms.

A trip here can easily be combined with a visit to the other factory stores just a few blocks away.

Fall River   *Clothing (Men's)*

DARWOOD MFG. CO., INC.
18 Pocasset Street
Tel. #617-675-7462
Monday-Friday 10:00-8:00
Saturday 9:00-5:00

Certainly the male members of the family should do very well at this factory store. There is a broad selection of slacks and outerwear for men and young men; certainly any budget with teen-age clothing needs included can use an assist! The choice of sizes, colors, and styles is ample.

This store is located only a few blocks from Battleship Cove; the opportunity to visit there should provide an added inducement.

Parking is certainly ample.

Fall River   *Clothing (Women's)*

FALL RIVER DRESS DISCOUNT CENTER
69 Alden Street
Tel. #617-673-4011
Monday, Tuesday, Saturday 10:00-5:00
Wednesday, Thursday, Friday 10:00-9:00

The Dress Discount Center has dresses, skirts, slacks, blouses, and pant suits in sizes from 14½ to 52. This is an especially attractive store for women needing larger sizes and looking for reasonably priced clothes. There is a nice assortment of styles and colors available.

Parking is ample and off the street.

Obviously, the fact that Fall River Knitting Mills is in the same complex makes the trip increasingly practical.

FALL RIVER KNITTING MILLS, INC.
69 Alden Street
Tel. #617-678-7553
Monday-Friday 9:00-9:00
Saturday 9:00-5:00

Fall River Knitting Mills has one of the best selection of sweaters for families of any of the factory stores. The range of styles, colors, and sizes should provide something for most any teen-ager through adults. There is a nice assortment of extra-large sizes for men, which is an added plus.

In addition to sweaters, there are jackets, slacks, and skirts for women, and some slacks and tops for toddlers.

To amuse young children, there are some interesting fish tanks.

The store is large, the merchandise is well displayed, and the sales clerks are most helpful.

Parking is ample and off the street. Everything combines to make this a delightful store!

Fall River   *Clothing*

FANTASTIC COAT FACTORY (Raincoat Outlet)
1637 North Main Street
Tel. #617-673-3289
Monday-Friday 9:30-9:00
Saturday 9:30-5:00
BankAmericard and Master Charge

This store has exactly what its name says - a fantastic display of coats! There is an excellent range of women's coats in a variety of fabrics, styles, sizes, and colors. A feature is the large assortment of raincoats, with the well known Boston Harbor Coats being a major attraction.

There are raincoats for men, also.

Parking is easy and ample; follow the signs from the parking area to the store.

KRAVIF FACTORY OUTLET
135 Alden Street
Tel. #617-678-5636
Saturday 8:00-12:00

Kravif's offers a fine selection of women's sportswear in sizes ranging from 6 to 20. Slacks, tops, pant suits, and some dresses will be found in an ample selection of styles and colors.

Note this store is open only on Saturday mornings. A portion of the factory floor itself is utilized for the display of merchandise, and it is not practical to do this during normal operating hours.

SHOE FACTORY OUTLET
1637 North Main Street
Tel. #617-673-3289
Monday-Friday 9:30-9:00
Saturday 9:30-5:00

Housed in the same building and on the same floor as the Fantastic Coat Factory, this store has an excellent assortment of name brand women's shoes. The range of sizes, styles, and colors is excellent.

The store is large, and parking, obviously, is the same as for the Coat Factory. Too bad more factory stores don't share facilities; it does simplify the shopping trips.

WOLFE LAMP FACTORY OUTLET
Wolfe Lamp Corp. of Mass.
18 Martine Street
Tel. #617-678-7561
Monday-Thursday 10:00-5:00
Friday 10:00-9:00
Saturday 10:00-4:00

This outlet offers a wide selection of lighting merchandise, including floor lamps, table lamps, ceiling fixtures, and lamp shades. A variety of styles is available, with choices ranging from colonial to modern. Some unusual styles are to be found; one featured recently uses a continuing flow of droplets of oil to simulate falling rain.

If you are redecorating and need lamps, a visit here should be worthwhile.

Fitchburg   *Shoes (Family)*

THOM McAN FACTORY OUTLET
John Fitch Highway
Tel. #617-342-0782
Monday-Saturday 10:00-5:00
Friday till 9:00

See Dover, New Hampshire listing.

Framingham   *Clothing (Men's)*

T. I. SWARTZ, CLOTHIERS
2nd Floor of Deerskin Trading Post
Route 9
Monday-Saturday 10:00-9:00
BankAmericard and Master Charge

See Peabody, Massachusetts listing.

Framingham   *Men & Women Sport Shoes*
                                Sport Clothes

EATON FACTORY OUTLET
44 Dinsmore Ave.

Tuesday-Saturday 9:00-5:00
Fridays until 9:00
Master Charge

Featuring factory-irregulars, samples, and
discontinued styles of men's and women's
Famous/Name golf and tennis shoes by Eaton. Also
a good selection of boating shoes and men's dress,
work, and casual shoes. Golf and tennis sportswear
by Eaton are also in good supply.

Gardner   *Home Furnishings*

BARRON'S BARN
126 South Main Street
Tel. #617-632-6285
Tuesday, Wednesday & Saturday 10:00-5:00
Thursday and Friday 12:00-9:00
Master Charge

Here you will find a complete selection of home
furnishings with good discounts. They have dining
room and kitchen tables and chairs, complete
bedroom sets, mattresses and box springs,
upholstered living room furniture, coffee and end
tables. As an added feature they also have lamps, all
types of accessories and many nice gift items. Good
quality here.

Gardner   *Furniture*

THE FACTORY STORE, INC.
90 Mechanic Street
Tel. #617-632-2401
Monday-Saturday 9:00-5:00

Featured here is the traditionally styled "early American" furniture. An excellent selection of pieces is available with chairs, deacon's benches, and Boston rockers being among those pieces considered typical of New England.
Well worth a trip!

Haverhill   *Luggage*

SAVOY ATTACHE CASE & LUGGAGE OUTLET
Savoy Leather Mfg.

Haverhill   *Luggage*

SAVOY ATTACHE CASE &
LUGGAGE OUTLET
Savoy Leather Mfg.
Industrial Park (off Route 495)
Neck Road
Tel. #617-374-0351
Monday-Thursday 9:00-4:00
Friday 9:00-3:00

A nice assortment of attache cases and luggage pieces will be found here. For gifts or for personal use, it would seem that almost everyone's taste would be satisfied. Style and color choices are adequate, and no one pressures you to make your decision in a hurry.

A nice place to shop!

Haverhill   *Coats (Leathers)*

SNYDER LEATHER FACTORY OUTLET
Railroad Square
Tel. #617-372-4481
Monday-Saturday 9:00-5:00
Tuesday and Friday till 9:00
BankAmericard and Master Charge

See Brighton, Massachusetts listing.

Holyoke   *Clothing (Women's)*

ELCO DRESS COMPANY FACTORY OUTLET
532 Main Street
Tel. #413-534-3767
Saturday only 9:30-3:00

The Elco Outlet features the products of a
nationally known 20 plant manufacturer, so an
excellent selection of women's clothing including
pant suits, blouses, shells, tops, and dresses is
available. The wide range of sizes, including 6
through 20, and 14½ through 24½, the choice of
styles and colors, and the excellent savings make a
trip here most worthwhile.

Note this outlet is only open on Saturdays.

Hyannis   *Clothing (Women's)*

KITTERY MILLS OF HYANNIS
585 Main Street
Tel. #617-775-6122
Sunday-Saturday 10:00-5:30
Friday till 8:00

See Kittery, Maine listing.

Lawrence   *Bedspreads*

BEDSPREAD MILL OUTLET
244 Broadway
Tel. #617-685-2303

See New Bedford, Massachusetts listing.

CONVERSE RUBBER COMPANY
Tel. #617-322-1500
Monday-Saturday 8:30-5:00

BRANCH STORES:
Route 28
Andover, Massachusetts
Tel. #617-475-5300
Monday-Saturday 8:30-5:00

Buttonwood Street
Bristol, Rhode Island
Tel. #401-253-6201
Monday-Saturday 8:30-5:00

An extensive selection of footwear for all members of the family will be found here. Everything from sneakers to sport shoes to waders to after-ski boots are available in an excellent range of sizes.

A visit here should be helpful, particularly if you are looking for sports oriented footwear.

Mansfield   *Giftware*

THE SILVER SHOP
South Main Street
Tel. # - None listed
Monday-Friday 9:30-12:00, 12:30-3:30

   The Silver Shop offers an excellent assortment of
silver and crystal items, including samples, excess
inventory, and discontinued items. The selection is
ample and sure to yield that "just right" gift for a
wedding or special occasion.
   Note the store is closed for lunch time.

Milford   *Coats (Men's, Women's)*

ANTHONY ROBERTS, INC.
45 Sumner Street
Tel. #617-473-7731
Monday-Saturday 9:00-5:00
BankAmericard and Master Charge

BRANCH STORES:
Route 1
North Attleboro, Massachusetts
Tel. #617-695-3711

Route 3A
210 Daniel Webster Highway
Nashua, New Hampshire
Tel. #603-888-0722

Anthony Roberts offers an excellent assortment of all-weather coats for men and women. The choice of styles, colors, and sizes is ample.

Sales personnel are very helpful, parking is ample, these factors combined with the savings make a trip here financially worthwhile and a pleasant shopping stop.

Needham   *Clothing (Men's, Women's,*
                                        Children's)

CALVERTS'
938 Highland Avenue
Tel. #617-444-8000
Monday-Friday 9:00-10:00
Saturday 9:00-5:30
Master Charge

This is an almost unbelievable "department store" of clothing for all members of the family, and it is offered at factory prices. Featured, of course, are Carter's clothes for infants and children: the breadth of offerings for all members of the family has to put this store in the special category.

If you haven't been to this store, and you are in the general area, a trip should be extremely worthwhile. The choices are sure to please everyone!

BEDSPREAD MILL OUTLET
21 Cove Street
Tel. #617-992-6600
Monday-Friday 10:00-5:00
Saturday 10:00-1:00
Thursday evening 6:00-9:00

BRANCH STORES:
133 Mathewson Street
Providence, Rhode Island
Tel. #401-861-9536

244 Broadway
Lawrence, Massachusetts
Tel. #617-685-2303

An excellent assortment of bedspreads is available here. Both woven and quilted types are to be found with styles ranging from colonial to modern. There is an excellent choice of sizes and fabrics.

Also to be found are some very interesting needlepoint kits.

If you are redecorating a bedroom, a trip here should be most satisfactory.

New Bedford   *Fabrics (Curtains & Drapes)*

BERKSHIRE HATHAWAY, INC.
Gifford Street
Tel. #617-993-7028
Monday-Saturday 10:00-4:45

The Berkshire Hathaway store has a nice
assortment of curtain and drapery fabrics as well as
ready-made curtains and drapes. The available
lengths should meet most needs; there is also a good
selection of fabrics and colors.

Parking is available in the factory parking lot.
There are several other stores within a few blocks,
so a trip here can cover a variety of needs.

New Bedford   *Nightwear (Women's,*
                                     Children's)

BONNIE LANE PAJAMA FACTORY OUTLET
Bonnie Lane Pajama Mfg. Company
Acushnet Ave. - Corner Wamsutta Street
Tel. #617-996-6763
Daily during factory hours

A climb to the third floor of this factory outlet not
only allows you to purchase children's and women's
sleepwear at a savings, but gives you an over-view
of production in a clothing mill. The merchandise
may be selected from cartons displayed in the work
area.

Certainly an interesting place to visit.

CAPE COD CLOTHING COMPANY
1 Coffin Avenue
Tel. #617-996-6746
Monday-Friday 1:00-4:00
Saturday 8:00-12:00

The Cape Cod factory store is solely for the men of the family. To be found here are suits and sport coats. A good selection is available, with a nice range of sizes and colors.

There is adequate parking; if you are combining a trip here with other factory stores in New Bedford, be sure to note that Cape Cod does not open until 1:00 during the week, and that it closes at noon on Saturday.

CLOVER BAY RETAIL OUTLET
102 North Front Street
Tel. #617-999-1255
Monday-Saturday 10:00-5:00
Friday till 9:00

BRANCH STORE:
BARGAIN HUNTERS
650 Branch Avenue
Providence, Rhode Island
Tel. #401-721-2207
Monday-Saturday 10:00-5:00
Thursday and Friday till 9:00

The Clover Bay Outlet is located in a new building
which is attractive and spacious.

There is an excellent selection of pants, tops,
skirts, long skirts, blouses, dresses, and pant suits.
The choice of sizes, styles, and colors is quite good,
and the selection of sportswear is really quite ample.

This is definitely a very attractive factory store.
The new building, the ample selection, the helpful
sales personnel, and the off-street parking are all
contributing factors.

DARTMOUTH TEXTILE REMNANT SHOP
Cove Street
Tel. # - None
Monday-Friday 8:00-4:00
Saturday 8:00-3:30

This Remnant Shop offers one of the best
selections of yard goods. The store is large and the
material is neatly displayed. If you are a quilter or
have some particular need for smaller quantities of
printed fabrics, this is probably the store offering
one of the nicest assortments at very reasonable
prices. Really, anyone who sews, and who is
planning a shopping trip to New Bedford, would
probably find a stop here worthwhile.

New Bedford   *Clothing (Girl's)*

EASTERN SPORTSWEAR FACTORY OUTLET
94 Sawyer Street
Tel. #617-999-5252
Tuesday-Saturday 11:00-5:00
Thursday till 9:00

Eastern Sportswear offers an excellent assortment of girls' sportswear and play wear. Their sizes are 2-4, 3-6X, and 7-14, and slacks, pants suits, and jeans are to be found in textured polyester, corduroy, and denim.

Anyone with young girls should find it practical to shop here as the selection is quite good.

If you are planning a trip here in conjunction with other stores, note that Eastern Sportswear does not open until 11:00. Plan your itinerary accordingly.

This store does close for a vacation period in July, so be sure to check before traveling any distance.

There is ample parking.

ELCO DRESS FACTORY STORE
330 Collette Street
Tel. #617-999-5629
Friday 5:00-8:30
Saturday 9:30-3:00

Although the Elco Factory Store is only open
Friday evening and Saturday, it does offer a good
selection of dresses, long dresses, pant suits, and
slacks in both half sizes and regular sizes. Sizes go
from 14 - 24½ and from 6-20 offering a broad
spectrum. To find larger sizes in a choice of styles
and colors is always a decided plus.

Just remember to plan your trip to New Bedford
on Friday or Saturday if you wish to include this
store in your shopping tour.

FAIRHAVEN CORPORATION
FACTORY OUTLET
358 Belleville Avenue
Tel. #617-993-9981
Monday-Friday 9:00-3:30
Saturday 9:00-2:00

The Fairhaven Outlet is located upstairs in a typical mill building. There is a certain charm to all of the older mills, as there is to this one.

A fine selection of handbags will be found in a nicely set up store area of the mill floor. There is an excellent choice of styles and colors, with both first quality and irregulars from which to choose. Most are of man-made materials, but some leather has been available.

An excellent place for Christmas shopping, for you should be able to find a purse for almost anyone on your list.

The salesperson is most helpful, and there is ample off-street parking.

HANDBAG OUTLET
21 Cove Street
Tel. # - None
Monday-Friday 10:00-4:00
Saturday 10:00-12:00

The Handbag Outlet offers a very nice selection of handbags in a wide variety of styles and colors. One of the features of this store is the opportunity to request a particular style handbag in any of their available colors if it is not on display. Every effort is made to be helpful in meeting particular needs, and if an item is available from the stock supply, they will gladly get it for you.

New Bedford   *Clothing (Men's)*
                                                Fabric

PIERCE MILL FACTORY OUTLET
419 Sawyer Street
Tel. #617-999-4033
Monday-Friday 11:30-9:00
Saturday 10:00-6:00
BankAmericard and Master Charge

   The Pierce Mill Outlet is a very large factory store
offering an extensive selection of men's suits, sport
coats, and slacks. Both first quality and irregular
items will be found, with the latter clearly marked.
   The selection of sizes, fabrics, and colors is
excellent, and certainly shopping here can give a
valuable boost to the clothing budget.
   There is also a large selection of fabrics and
related sewing needs, including a very large
assortment of buttons, available.
   With the extensive selection, helpful sales
personnel, a 30 day lay-a-way plan, and ample
parking, this is an excellent factory store.

REVERE COPPER AND BRASS, INC.
24 N. Front Street
Tel. #617-999-5601
Tuesday-Saturday 10:00-4:30

BRANCH STORE:
Lothrop Street
Plymouth
Tel. #617-746-1000
Monday-Saturday 9:30-5:00

At Revere's store, an excellent assortment of their famous cooking utensils is found. The copper bottom pots and pans or the all copper clad items will perk up anyone's kitchen. The copper is lovely, and any of the items would make desirable gifts.

Starter sets, single pieces, and specialty items

Starter sets, single pieces, and specialty items such as a Revere tie tac are all available.

Revere categorizes the items sold here as premium seconds, with the defect being a cosmetic blemish. To the untrained eye, most appear to be perfect.

This is a very attractive factory store, with a broad assortment of merchandise, helpful sales personnel, and adequate parking.

SLACKS AND TOPS
21 Cove Street
Tel. #617-997-0611
Tuesday-Friday 10:00-9:00
Saturday 10:00-1:00

This store offers a very fine selection of name
brand slacks, tops, sweaters, skirts, blouses, and
some night wear. There is an ample selection of sizes
and colors; if you are looking for sportswear, this
store is an excellent choice.

Some fabric remnants are also available.

This outlet shares a floor in the factory building
with the Bedspread Outlet, so you can plan a visit to
both; be sure to watch the closing times of each.

Newton   *China, Glass, Cookware*

CHINA FAIR WAREHOUSE
70 Needham Street
Tel. #617-332-1520
Monday-Saturday 9:00-5:00

   See Cambridge, Massachusetts listing.

North Attleboro   *Coats (Men's, Women's)*

ANTHONY ROBERTS, INC.
Route #1
Tel. #617-695-3711

   See Milford Massachusetts listing.

DANTE FACTORY OUTLET
544 Kelly Boulevard (Rte. 152)
Tel. # - None listed
Daily 10:00-5:00
Closes in summer
Master Charge

This store offers the complete line of Dante gift items for men. Cuff links, wallets, and all the small gift items such as men's jewelry boxes, belts, credit card cases, etc. are available here.

In addition, some jewelry items for women are also available.

Worth a visit!

550 COSTUME JEWELRY
550 Kelly Boulevard (Rte. 152)
Tel. # - None listed
Monday-Saturday 10:00-5:00
Sunday 1:00-5:00

This factory store carries an extensive line of costume jewelry. The latest items in this category are available, and are usually overruns or sales samples.

In addition, a nice variety of small gift items will be found here.

Easy to visit, and worth a shopping stop if you are a costume jewelry person.

North Attleboro   *Jewelry,*
Small Leather Goods

MANUFACTURER'S JEWELRY OUTLET
Kell Boulevard (Rte. 152)
Tel. # - None listed
Daily 10:00-5:00
BankAmericard and Master Charge

This large store features an excellent assortment
of jewelry for both men and women. Gold and silver
are available in most attractive designs. To be found
are necklaces, bracelets, pins, tie tacs, cuff links,
and other jewelry pieces. Also available have been
small leather goods such as wallets and charge card
cases.
Worth visiting!

North Attleboro   *Jewelry, Watches*

WELLS BENRUS FACTORY STORE
Kelly Boulevard (Route 152)
Tel. #617-695-1069
Monday-Saturday 9:00-5:00

An outstanding assortment of the Wells jewelry
line will be found here including earrings, charms,
bracelets, necklaces, and pins in both sterling silver
and gold filled. Men's jewelry including cuff links
and tie tacs, leather items such as wallets, and
Benrus watches are also available.
The wide selection and the ease of shopping make
this well worth a visit.

PINE TRADITIONS
666 State Road (Route 6)
Tel. #617-996-2236
Monday-Friday 10:00-4:00
Saturday and Sunday 10:00-5:00

This outlet store for the Sears Furniture Mfg. Co. offers a fine selection of solid pine furniture. The furniture is available in either the dark antiqued pine finish or the honey antiqued pine finish; if you are a do-it-yourself person, you may purchase the pieces unfinished and finish in your own choice.

Located between Fall River and New Bedford, it would be an easy stop to combine with a shopping trip to either place.

Parking is adequate.

NORTH OXFORD MILLS
Route 12
Tel. #617-987-8521
Monday-Saturday 9:00-5:00

Both broadloom and braided rugs are available with the possibility of having braided rugs made to order, if desired. An excellent selection of weights and colors will be found in the broadlooms, and the braided rugs are available in colors which should harmonize with most color schemes.

This is a very interesting mill to visit, with the sales personnel most helpful!

THORNDIKE MILLS, INC.
Ware Road, Route 32
1 mile north of Exit 8 Mass. Tpk.
Tel. #413-283-9021
Saturdays Only 9:00-12:00 Noon
Master Charge and BankAmericard

Quality Braided Rugs manufactured here in Palmer at the same location of the Mill Store. Both wools and synthetic fibers are used in the various patterns and designs manufactured. Offered at a substantial saving over retail prices are closeouts, overruns, offgrades, and trial run items. Sizes from scatter to 9x12 in heavy assortments. The selection is large and certainly more than adequate for most needs. For the truly colonial minded here is a source that offers the best in quality and assortment.

PLYMOUTH YARN COMPANY
11 Peabody Square
Tel. #617-532-0929

Featured at "low, low prices" is a good assortment of yarns including hand knitting, rug, and crewel weights in both wool and acrylic. The choice of colors is excellent and the low prices make a shopping trip here attractive to most crafts people.

Note it is necessary to call in advance.

Peabody   *Clothing (Men's)*

T. I. SWARTZ, CLOTHIERS
119 Foster Street
Tel. #617-531-1633
Monday-Saturday 10:00-6:00
Monday, Wednesday, Friday till 9:00
BankAmericard and Master Charge

BRANCH STORE:
2nd Floor of Deerskin Trading Post
Route 9
Framingham, Massachusetts
Monday-Saturday 10:00-9:00
BankAmericard and Master Charge

This outstanding store clearly spells out what you should be looking for in men's clothing as far as quality and detail is concerned.

Manufacturers of men's suits, they offer a Grade 4 suit (suits are graded 1, 2, 4, and 6, with the higher the grade, the better the quality) in a variety of styles including traditional, contemporary, European, and leisure, in both vested and unvested choices. Sizes range from 36 short to 50 extra-long; if what you need is not on the rack, it is possible to have a suit custom made.

The excellent selection, the helpful personnel, and the fine quality make this a store well worth visiting!

Pittsfield   *Clothing (Men's, Women's,*
                                              Children's)

CHARLESTOWN MILL STORE
316 Housatonic Street
Tel. #413-443-1467

See Charlestown, New Hampshire listing.

Plainville   *Jewelry*

BAUBLES LTD.
Route 1
Tel. #617-695-7662
Monday-Saturday 9:00-5:00
Master Charge

A most attractive assortment of distinctive
costume jewelry will be found here. The designs are
both unusual and the more traditional; there should
be something for almost everyone's taste.

Plainville   *Jewelry*

LeDOR
Route 1
Tel. #617-695-6842
Monday-Saturday 9:00-5:00
BankAmericard and Master Charge

A beautiful selection of jewelry and small gift
items is to be found in this very attractive shop.
Ranging from the everyday to the elegant, the
choice of jewelry is almost sure to please everyone.
Items for both men and women are available.

REVERE COPPER AND BRASS, INC.
Lothrop Street
Tel. #617-746-1000
Monday-Saturday 9:30-5:00

See New Bedford, Massachusetts listing.

PAIRPONT GLASS COMPANY
851 Sandwich Road
Tel. #617-888-2344
Sunday-Saturday 9:00-6:00
Blowing room open to visitors
Monday-Friday 9:00-4:30

This delightful shop offers a most educational experience for everyone interested in glass blowing, for it is possible to watch this process.

Offered in the salesroom are lovely handmade lead crystal vases, bowls, decanters, paperweights, candlesticks, and other gift items.

Definitely a unique and enjoyable shopping stop!

Salem   *Sweaters*

KARSON SWEATER MILL STORE
35 Congress Street Shetland Industrial Park
Tel. #617-745-0200
Monday-Saturday 10:00-5:30
Master Charge

Sweaters for men, women and children. Also very
nice to find are a generous number of king and queen
sizes. All at good savings.

Saugus   *Clothing (Maternity)*

DAN HOWAR'S MATERNITY
FACTORY OUTLET
Route 1 North (Augustine's Plaza)
Tel. #617-233-5254
Monday-Friday 10:00-9:00
Saturday 10:00-6:00
BankAmericard and Master Charge

Shops carrying maternity clothes seem to be few
and far between; to find a factory outlet carrying
them is a rarity, indeed!
The selection is delightful, and the styles are
suited to every occasion. If you are expecting, a
visit here should be most helpful; the styles are
most attractive, and help to make you feel
comfortably and attractively dressed.

Saugus   *Shoes (Family)*

THOM McAN FACTORY OUTLET
739 Broadway (Route 1)
Tel. #617-233-3933
Monday-Saturday 10:00-9:00

See Dover, New Hampshire listing.

Stoughton   *Footwear*

FACTORY SNEAKER OUTLET
43 Canton Street (Route 27)
Tel. #617-344-1617
Monday-Friday 9:30-6:00
Thursday and Friday till 8:00
Saturday 9:00-5:00

This outlet store offers an excellent assortment of footwear for men, women, and children. Included are sneakers and other sport shoes, snow boots, dress boots, stretch rubber boots, work shoes, and industrial footwear. The range of sizes and styles is ample; it would seem that the needs of the whole family could be satisfied in this footwear store.

TWIN-KEE CLOTHING MFG. CO.
720 Park Street (Route 27)
Tel. #617-344-4751
Monday-Friday 8:00-9:00
Saturday 8:00-6:00

Twin-Kee offers an excellent assortment of all-weather coats for all members of the family. A good selection of sizes and colors is available and both full length and three quarter length styles are to be found. Zip-in linings may be purchased separately.

The delightful sales personnel, the ease of parking, and the good selections are all factors which make a shopping trip here a pleasant experience.

Taunton   *Curtains, Drapes*

CURTAIN FACTORY OUTLET
42 Adams Street
Tel. #617-823-4196
Monday-Friday 9:30-5:00
Thursday till 8:00
Saturday 9:30-3:30

The Curtain Factory Outlet offers a very good
selection of curtains and drapes including Cape Cod,
Priscilla, and novelty styles. Fabrics, lengths, and
colors are to be found in a very adequate range.

In addition, there is a complete custom drapery
service available.

Taunton   *Clothing (Men's)*

WEIR FACTORY OUTLET
120 Ingell Street
Tel. #617-822-9456
Monday-Friday 10:00-9:00
Saturday 10:00-6:00
BankAmericard and Master Charge

An excellent assortment of men's sport coats,
suits, and slacks is available at the Weir Outlet
store. The range of sizes and colors is ample, and the
polyester fabric insures easy care.

In addition, a nice assortment of yard goods will
also be found here.

Uxbridge   *Fabrics, Yarns*

STANLEY-BERROCO, INC.
140 Mendon Street (Route 16)
Tel. #617-278-2451
Monday-Saturday 9:00-5:00
Master Charge

This is one of the most delightful stores listed! The helpfulness and the genuine friendliness of the people employed here set an atmosphere which can't be beat.

The fabrics are beautiful, and certainly are an enticement even to the non sewer. An excellent assortment of yarns is available, in a multitude of colors. Wool and synthetics, mohair, loop, and fisherman type are but a few of the varieties available.

There are coats and sweaters available in the ready-made category.

In addition to the two floors, there is also a cellar where imported yarns are featured, and "the barn" which contains an unbelievable amount of yarns.

Sewers, knitters, and the hand weavers will find this especially worthwhile. The mill itself is of historical interest; altogether, a trip here is just plain delightful! And if you are fortunate enough to have a tour of the mill, you will be intrigued by the process involved.

UXBRIDGE YARN MILL OUTLET
Route 16
Tel. #617-278-5611
Monday-Saturday 9:30-4:30

The yarns and kits of the well-known Bernat Company are offered here.

There is an excellent selection of knitting yarns and accessories available, including the up-to-date and specialty items. Various kits are also available.

An Annex is located downstairs and offers added bargains.

The ample quantity, the easy parking, and the helpful sales personnel are all factors which make a trip here well worthwhile.

FREDERIC'S MILL STORE
Route 32
Tel. #413-967-5631
Monday-Friday 9:00-5:00
Saturday 9:00-12:00

Frederic's offers a nice assortment of sweaters, panties, underwear, stockings, socks, children's pajamas, and knitwear. The selection of styles, sizes, and colors is certainly adequate.

Ware   *Shoes (Men's & Women's)*

PIONEER VALLEY SHOE OUTLET
East Street
Monday-Saturday 9:00-5:00
Master Charge and BankAmericard

In addition to a good feature on men's and
women's shoes, they have a nice selection of
handbags. Also they have a complete line of men's,
women's and children's sneakers.

Ware   *Fabrics*

WARE KNITTERS (Fabric)
Route 32 (Industry Yard)
Tel. #413-967-6261
Monday-Friday 9:00-4:15
Saturday 9:00-3:15

An extensive selection of bonded knit fabrics is
available at the Ware Knitters store. The choice of
colors and patterns is certainly ample; any sewer
should find several choices for any garment
planned.

Ware   *Clothing (Men's, Women's*
                                            Children's)

WARE KNITTERS (Garments)
Route 32 (Industry Yard)
Tel. #413-967-6261
Monday-Friday 9:00-4:15
Saturday 9:00-3:15

An excellent assortment of clothing for adults
and children will be found here. Skirts, shirts,
blouses, tops, slacks, dresses, and some lightweight
windbreakers are available, with a good range of
sizes, colors, and styles.

Easy parking and the nice selection should make
your shopping trip here successful.

Ware   *Fabrics*

WARE METALS REMNANT NOOK
East Street
Tel. #413-697-6276
Monday-Friday 8:00-4:45
Saturday 8:00-11:45

The selection of fabrics and remnants offered here
makes this a worthwhile trip for the home sewer. A
wide range of fabrics is offered, and although the
store is small, it would seem to be a store worth
visiting.

WARE SPORTS WEAR
Route 32 (Industry Yard)
Tel. #413-967-5964
Monday-Friday 9:00-5:00
Saturday 9:00-1:00

Ware Sports Wear offers an excellent assortment
of women's clothing, including skirts, jackets,
slacks, and culotte skirts in the latest styles and
colors. The fabrics vary with the season, of course.

Certainly worth a visit! The selection, the helpful
sales personnel, the easy parking, and the savings
all combine to make a visit here usually successful.

Ware   *Fabrics*

WEDGMOOR WOOLENS
Route 32
Tel. #413-967-6227
Monday-Friday 8:00-5:00
Saturday 8:00-3:00
BankAmericard

Numerous bolts of woolen and acrylic fabrics,
both bonded and unbonded, are available in the
Wedgmoor store. The variety is large, and would
seem to fit the woolen needs of just about any
seamstress. Yarn is also on sale here, and lately
have been added a few cottons and notions.

The store shares the Ware area with several other
factory stores, so a trip to one should include a trip
to the rest of the complex, and, of course, should
result in most impressive savings.

MAR DEL MANUFACTURING
Corner Main & North Streets
Tel. #413-436-7643
Monday-Friday 9:00-4:00
Saturday 9:00-1:00

Mar Del carries an impressive assortment of children's knits in a good selection of sizes and colors. Skirts, slacks, tops, bathing outfits in season, and dresses are to be found.

If you have young children, a trip here will be worthwhile. The styles are always current, and the savings should be helpful to the clothing budget.

West Warren *Fabric, Trims*

WRIGHTS IDEA CENTER MILL STORE
Main Street (Route 67)
Tel. #413-436-7732
Monday-Friday 8:00-4:00
Saturday 8:30-12:00

The Mill Store is delightful and chock full of bargains! The entire line of trims and other sewing items manufactured by Wrights is available.

Rick rack, bias binding, dozens of styles of decorative trims, ball fringe, metallic type trims, lace trims, seam binding, bows, and some fabrics are but a partial listing of the available stock.

If you are a sewer, a crafts person, or even just a browser, a trip here should be extremely worthwhile. In addition to the extensive stock, the off street parking and the extremely helpful sales personnel are added assets.

An interesting sewing machine museum is also to be found here.

Webster   *Footwear (Men's, Women's)*

LITTLE RED SHOE HOUSE
South Main Street
Tel. # - Unlisted
Monday-Saturday 9:00-5:00

The Little Red Shoe House offers an excellent assortment of footwear for men, women, and children. Dress and casual styles are available, as are boots, sneakers, and sport shoes. The range of sizes and styles is certainly ample.

In addition, handbags, some children's clothes, stockings, and gloves are available.

SHERWOOD FACTORY GIFT STORE
Route 10 & 202
Tel. #413-562-5851
Monday-Friday 9:00-5:00
Thursday and Friday till 9:00
Sunday 11:00-5:00

BRANCH STORE:
1805 Berlin Turnpike
Wethersfield, Connecticut
Tel. #203-563-2659
Monday-Friday 11:00-7:00
Saturday and Sunday 11:00-5:00

This factory gift store carries an extensive line of
giftware priced at factory prices. Hundreds of items
including colonial accessories, china, housewares,
planters, area rugs, framed prints, a complete line of
doll house furniture, and innumerable other
categories are to be found. The items are
attractively displayed, and the prices are a boon to
the gift budget.

ARTS & CRAFTS FACTORY
OUTLET SUPPLIES
Worcester South Plaza (Grafton Street)
Tel. #617-753-9581
Sunday-Tuesday 10:00-6:00
Wednesday-Saturday 10:00-9:00
BankAmericard and Master Charge

This factory outlet offers an extensive variety of
arts and crafts supplied from Lee Wards and other
arts and crafts companies at substantial savings. A
broad range of crafts including glassware,
needlepoint, decoupage, 3D art, candles, sequin
fruit, etc. is covered, with both materials and kits
available.

An interesting place to visit.

Worcester   *Clothing (Men's, Boy's)*

DJ'S FACTORY OUTLET
75 Harding Street
Tel. #617-755-2022
Monday-Friday 9:30-5:00
Wednesday till 9:00
Sunday 10:00-5:00
Master Charge

   DJ's offers an excellent assortment of shirts, ties,
slacks, jackets, and sweaters for men and boys. The
range of styles, colors, and sizes should make a
shopping trip here a worthwhile experience for the
male members of the family.
   With Heywood and DJ's on the same street, a
shopping trip to Harding Street should be very
rewarding.

HEYWOOD FACTORY SHOWROOM
85 Harding Street
Tel. #617-755-0745
Wednesday-Friday 10:00-5:30
Sunday 10:00-5:00
BankAmericard and Master Charge

This large store features an outstanding selection of raincoats, sportswear, sweaters, and separates for women and juniors. The choice of sizes, colors, and styles is certainly ample. Surely there is something for practically everyone in the Heywood Showroom.

A successful shopping trip should be the result of a visit here.

KUNIN FABRICS MILL STORE
Brussels Street
Tel. #617-755-1241
Monday-Friday 9:00-5:00

An excellent selection of fabrics and felt is available at the Kunin Store. For the home sewer, the varied assortment will be a delight, and for the craft person or teacher, the selection of felt is sure to be well worth a trip!

The store has moved from the Thomas Street location; be sure to note the current address.

Worcester   *Clothing (Women's)*

THE SLOVIN COMPANY
Higgins Industrial Park
Tel. #617-853-4289
Monday-Friday 10:00-5:00
Saturday 10:00-12:00

The Slovin Company offers a good selection of women's sportswear, including slacks, skirts, and shorts. Ranging in size from 4 to 16, and in an ample selection of colors it would seem that most everyone could shop successfully here.

The sales personnel are most helpful, making a trip here a pleasant experience.

THOMAS TURNER COMPANY, INC.
Off Route 5
Tel. #802-463-3366
Friday, Saturday, Sunday, and holidays 10:00-4:00

The newly opened factory outlet store of the Thomas Turner Company offers an extensive line of Vermont Pine cocktail tables, end tables, small cabinets, trestle dining tables and benches, all first quality. In addition, composite items with Formica or vinyl tops, which includes T.V. folding tables, stack tables, game tables, cocktail tables, and end tables are also available.

Seconds and factory defect items are offered, as well as the first quality merchandise.

A trip here for furniture would seem to be most worthwhile. The selection is excellent, and everyone is most helpful. Often, visitors are treated to a most worthwhile factory tour.

Bennington   *Giftwrap*

THE BEN-MONT STORE
Ben Mont Avenue
Tel. #802-442-6331
Sunday-Saturday 12:00-5:00
July 6-December 24

After you've visited all the factory stores, and
purchased treasures galore, a final stop at the Ben-
Mont Store will provide you with all the gift
wrapping paper in which to wrap them. Both
everyday patterns as well as Christmas designs are
available here in a very good selection. Flat folds,
single rolls, and multi-pack rolls are all available in
designs ranging from traditional to the
sophisticated. Foils, tissue, kraft paper, and regular
paper are all available.

In addition, items such as bows, greeting cards,
and Christmas tinsel are available.

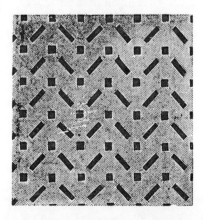

BENNINGTON POTTERS
324 County Street
Tel. #802-447-7531
Monday-Saturday 8:30-5:30
Sunday 12:00-5:30
Summer only Monday-Saturday 8:00-8:00
Tours Monday-Friday at 2:15
Master Charge

The Bennington Potters store is chock full of a wide array of mugs, dinnerware, and home accessories. For anyone who enjoys the look of stoneware, this is an outstanding place to shop. The distinctive Bennington mark will be found on the underside of the pieces, helping to identify future heirlooms.

Overruns, discontinued items, and seconds are all available. Pitchers, banks, ashtrays, special mugs, and dishes are to be found, making both shopping for yourself and for gifts an easy experience.

Other shops in the yard, as well as other factory stores in the same area, help to make a trip here a most enjoyable one.

Bennington   *Clothing (Men's, Women's,*
Children's)

CHARLESTOWN MILL STORE
112 Northside Drive
Tel. #802-447-7722

See Charlestown, New Hampshire listing.

Bennington   *Sweaters*

WAGON WHEEL WOOLENS
North and Adams Streets (Route 7)
Tel. #802-442-5639
Open every day
BankAmericard and Master Charge

The Wagon Wheel Woolens does indeed look like
a "supermarket of sweaters." A wide assortment of
sweaters for everyone in an extensive selection of
sizes, styles, and colors insures a very good choice;
in addition, there are blankets, jackets, gloves,
mufflers, mittens, caps, and other items of apparel.
It would seem that a trip here could be most helpful
to the clothing budget.

Brattleboro *Clothing (Men's, Women's, Children's)*

CHARLESTOWN MILL STORE
Putney Road
Tel. #802-257-0742

See Charlestown, New Hampshire listing.

Brattleboro *Handbags, Small Leather Goods*

FACTORY HANDBAG STORE
Canal Street (Route 5)
Tel. #802-254-4594
Seven days a week 9:00-9:00

The Factory Store carries an extensive line of handbags in a variety of styles and colors, as well as a very wide selection of men's and women's wallets, deerskin moccasins and gloves, and leather belts.

If you are traveling north to Vermont, this store is located at Exit 1 off I-91, making a nice stop for a change of pace from driving.

Burlington   *Giftware (Wooden)*

J. K. ADAMS CO., INC.
137 College Street
Potters North Building
Tel. #802-658-6730
Monday-Saturday 9:00-5:00
Friday till 9:00

   See Dorset, Vermont listing.

Burlington   *Clothing (Men's, Women's,*
                                Children's)

CHARLESTOWN MILL STORE
1690 Williston Road
Tel. #802-862-1849

Shelburne Road - Route 7
Tel. #802-985-8564

   See Charlestown, New Hampshire listing.

KENNEDY BROTHERS, INC.
Corner of Church and
College Streets
Tel. #802-862-7393
Monday-Saturday 9:00-5:30
Friday till 9:00

See Vergennes, Vermont listing.

J. K. ADAMS CO., INC.
Route 30
Tel. #802-362-2303
Monday-Friday 8:00-5:30
Saturday 9:30-5:30
Sunday (summer) 11:00-5:30

BRANCH STORE:
137 College Street
Potters North Building
Burlington
Tel. #802-658-6730
Monday-Saturday 9:00-5:00
Friday till 9:00

One of the most beautiful assortments of wooden items will be found at the J. K. Adams store. Their complete line is on display and includes ice chests, Lazy Susans, coasters, cheese boards, carving boards, knife racks, spice racks, chess and checker boards, measuring rules, small containers, butcher block tables, and a variety of other items.

If you are a wood worker, pieces of wood are sometimes available.

If you need kindling, bundles of it may also be found here.

The items include first quality, factory seconds, close outs and discontinued items, and pilot and test runs of new products.

Whether you are looking for a gift or something for yourself, if you are a lover of wooden items, this should be a worthwhile shop to visit.

GRANVILLE MANUFACTURING CO., INC.
Route 100
Tel. #802-767-8961
Monday-Friday 7:00-12:00, 1:00-4:00

An excellent selection of wooden bowls will be found at this factory store.

If you are traveling in New England, and want a reminder of your trip, these bowls are an ideal choice.

Granville   *Giftware*

JeMEL WOOD PRODUCTS
Route 100
Tel. #802-767-3266
7 days a week 8:00-6:00
BankAmericard

An interesting variety of wooden gift items is available in this delightful shop. Those items of wood such as sconces, candle holders, bowls, and other serving accessories identified as seconds by the manufacturer are featured.

Other Vermont gift items are also available; these, however, are offered at regular retail prices.

VERMONT WOOD SPECIALTIES
Route 100
Tel. #802-767-5237
Daily 8:00-5:00

Factory seconds of the wooden giftware manufactured here include cheeseboards, Lazy Susans, condiment sets, ice buckets, and bowls will be found here. The selection is quite extensive. Other Vermont gift items will be found here, but the savings are offered only on the items manufactured here.

Johnson   *Blankets, Clothing (Woolen)*

JOHNSON WOOLEN MILLS
Route 15
Tel. #802-635-2271
Monday-Friday 8:00-5:00
Seasonal only - Saturday 9:00-4:00

An excellent assortment of all wool blankets, as well as hunting clothes, coats, scarves, yard goods, and remnants, is to be found here. The blankets include baby blankets, single, double, queen, and king sizes, camp blankets, and car robes. The choice of colors should be more than adequate for almost every shopper.

TONI TOTES OF VERMONT
Route 100
Tel. #802-824-3520
Open Sunday-Saturday 10:00-5:00

The Toni Tote Factory Store offers their complete line of canvas and fabric handbags, totes, and luggage. Also to be found are preassembled totes for needlepoint inserts, as well as pillows, lucite, and wooden accessories for needle work. The Totepoint kits are unique to Toni.

There is always an excellent selection of the Toni line. A visit here should prove to be worthwhile.

MANCHESTER WOODCRAFT
Routes 11 and 30
Tel. # - None listed
Daily 8:30-5:30

This delightful store has available an extensive array of wooden items. There are cutting boards in a wide choice of shapes, buckets, ladder-back chairs, bar stools, rocking chairs, toy trucks, cribbage boards, doll house furniture scaled 1″ to 1′, and various other intriguing items. Also available are reproduction tin candle molds and pierced tin lampshades.

the items may be purchased finished or unfinished.

If you like to make your own toys, etc., there is an excellent assortment of wood turnings available.

The store is delightful and full of treasures!

SWEATERTOWN, U.S.A.
Route 4
Tel. #802-773-7358

See Rutland, Vermont listing.

Middlebury   *Clothing (Men's, Women's,*
                                                Children's)

CHARLESTOWN MILL STORE
Route 7 South
Tel. #802-388-4800

   See Charlestown, New Hampshire listing.

Pownal   *Clothing (Men's, Women's, Children's)*

CHARLESTOWN MILL STORE
Route 7
Tel. #802-823-5060

   See Charlestown, New Hampshire listing.

SWEATERTOWN, U.S.A.
Route 7 (Mill Village)
Tel. #802-775-1333
Open 7 days a week

An excellent assortment of sweaters and sportswear will be found here. There is a broad range of sizes and colors for the entire family. The store also carries Vermont maple syrup, cheeses, and souvenirs; the savings will be found only on the sweaters and sportswear.

COLONIAL VERMONT, INC.
Route 7
Tel. #802-985-2742
Monday-Saturday 9:00-5:00
BankAmericard and Master Charge

An excellent assortment of pine furniture will be found here. Almost anything you can think of is available; if you'd like a specially designed piece this can probably be made. The selection is certainly sure to provide something for almost anyone who appreciates the special warmth of pine.

The delightful sales personnel and the selection are factors which make a trip here an enjoyable experience.

Stowe   *Giftware (Wooden)*

KENNEDY BROTHERS, INC.
Route 100, Stowe Village
Tel. #802-253-8006
Sunday-Saturday, Hours vary with season

See Vergennes, Vermont listing.

MARY MEYER FACTORY STORE
Route 30
Tel. #802-365-7793
Sunday-Saturday 9:00-5:00

The advertising says "the woods in Townshend are full of tigers;" one might well add "and teddies and turtles and every other animal imaginable!" The stuffed toys are absolutely enchanting, with the psychedelic colors of rose, chartreuse, and orange vying with the checkerboards, the checks, and the more traditional, subdued pinks and blues. There are musical stuffed toys, hand puppets, and a variety of other choices in the Noah's Ark collection, surely something for everyone!

The store is again enlarging, so even more items will be on display.

The peaceful setting, the large variety of choice, and the enchantment of the appealing toys, make this a delightful place to shop.

TOWNSHEND FURNITURE CO., INC.
Route 30
Tel. #802-365-7720
Monday-Friday 9:00-10:00
Saturday and Sunday 10:00-5:00

BRANCH STORE:
Route 44
New Hartford, Connecticut
Tel. #203-379-4341
Tuesday-Saturday 10:00-5:00
Sunday 12:00-5:00
Master Charge

If your choice of furniture style is pioneer or early New England, shopping in this store will be a delight!

Largely handmade from native lumber, the furniture is well constructed and beautifully finished. Sofas, chairs, tables, hutches, mirrors, coffee tables, chests, desks, end tables, and accessories are all to be found.

The extensive selection of the lovely traditional furniture, the easy parking, and the helpful sales personnel, all combine to make a trip here a delightful shopping experience.

KENNEDY BROTHERS, INC.
11 Main Street
Tel. #802-877-2975
Sunday-Saturday 8:30-5:00
Extended in summer.
Factory — Monday-Friday only
BankAmericard and Master Charge

BRANCH STORES:
Corner of Church and College Streets
Burlington
Tel. #802-862-7393
Monday-Saturday 9:00-5:30
Friday till 9:00

Route 100
Stowe Village, Stowe
Tel. #802-253-8006
Sunday-Saturday, Hours vary with season

This is a very extensive gift store, offering everything from furniture to glassware. The items made at Kennedy Brothers are the wooden items, such as salad bowls, cutting boards, trays, buckets, and so on. The entire process from log to finished product is executed in Vermont. You will find first quality, discontinued, and second quality in the available woodenware.

It is possible to view the manufacturing process through three large picture windows.

This is truly a delightful factory store and an impressive giftshop! Savings are only on the items manufactured here.

WESTON BOWL MILL AND ANNEX
Route 100
Tel. #802-824-6219
Monday-Saturday 9:00-5:00
Sunday 11:00-5:00

The Bowl Mill and Annex are "manufacturers and
purveyors of the finest in quality woodenware,
manufactured on the premises and elsewhere in
Vermont, and offered at Mill Prices." The variety of
woodenware is almost overwhelming with something for everyone to be found. Certainly one could
easily find a gift for just about anyone here.

HARTFORD WOOLEN CO., INC.
Woolen Wonderland
Junction Routes 5 and 4
Tel. #802-295-3645
9:00-5:00 7 days May-January
(extended hours in summer)
BankAmericard and Master Charge

BRANCH STORE:
Mount Cardigan Woolens
Bristol, New Hampshire
Tel. #603-744-2951
9:00-5:00 7 days June-October

Featured at this gift shop are the lovely woolen
sportswear and woolen fabrics manufactured by the
Hartford Woolen Co., Inc. Shirts, jackets, skirts,
and capes are among the items offered, in an ample
range of colors and sizes. The fabrics are certainly
attractive, and if you sew, will definitely be
tempting.

Bristol   *Fabric, Clothing (Woolen)*

MOUNT CARDIGAN WOOLENS
Bristol
Tel. #603-744-2951
Open 7 days 9:00-5:00 June-October

See White River Junction, Vermont - Hartford
Woolen Co., Inc. listing.

Charlestown   *Clothing (Men's, Women's,
                                              Children's)*

CHARLESTOWN MILL STORE
Main Street
Tel. #603-826-7788
Monday-Saturday 9:00-9:00
Sunday 10:00-5:00
BankAmericard and Master Charge

112 Northside Drive   Shelburne Road-Route 7
Bennington, Vermont   Burlington, Vermont
Tel. #802-447-7722   Tel. #802-985-8564

Route 7   316 West Housatonic Street
Pownal, Vermont   Pittsfield, Massachusetts
Tel. #802-823-5060   Tel. #413-443-1467

Route 7 South   East Pleasant Street
Middlebury, Vermont   Amherst, Massachusetts
Tel. #802-388-4800   Tel. #413-549-6670

Putney Road   120 Main Street
Brattleboro, Vermont   Keene, New Hampshire
Tel. #802-257-0742   Tel. #603-352-2101

1690 Williston Road
Burlington, Vermont
Tel. #802-862-1849

In addition to the advertised 20,000 sweaters, the
Charlestown Mill Stores offer a wide variety of
clothing, including slacks, tops, shorts, shirts,
men's jackets, and slacks, and children's slacks and
tops. The selection is always ample, with seasonal
sales being especially helpful to the budget.

Concord   *Paints and Stains*

FLETCHER'S PAINT WORKS
76 North Main Street
Tel. #603-225-2198
Monday-Thursday 8:30-5:30
Friday till 9:00
Saturday 9:00-5:00
BankAmericard and Master Charge

See Milford, New Hampshire listing.

Conway   *Fabric*

WHITE MOUNTAIN WOOLENS
Route #16
Tel. #603-447-2443
Sunday-Saturday 9:00-5:00

The White Mountain Woolens store offers "New England Woolens at mill prices". An excellent assortment of woolen fabric by the yard, rug wool, remnants, and yarns will be found here.

Sewers, knitters, rug makers, and others interested in needlework will all find something here.

Dover   *Shoes (Family)*

THOM McAN FACTORY OUTLET
385 Central Avenue
Tel. #603-742-2633
Monday-Saturday 10:00-5:00
Friday till 9:00

345 Main Street
Manchester
Tel. #603-623-8024
Monday-Saturday 9:00-5:00
Thursday till 9:00

Lord Pont Plaza
Athol, Massachusetts
Tel. #617-249-3395
Monday-Saturday 10:00-5:00
Thursday till 9:00
Closed Wednesday

739 Broadway (Route 1)
Saugus, Massachusetts
Tel. #617-233-3933
Monday-Saturday 10:00-9:00

9 Spruce Street
Nashua
Tel. #603-889-6108
Monday-Saturday
9:00-5:00
Thursday till 9:00

John Fitch Highway
Fitchburg
Massachusetts
Tel. #617-342-0782
Monday-Saturday
10:00-5:00
Friday till 9:00

The Thom McAn outlet offers shoes for the
family. These are slight irregulars; anyone buying
shoes for children can appreciate that after the first
day of wearing, almost anyone would be hard
pressed to determine the irregularity from the day's
bruises. Certainly a good variety of shoes for all
family members will be found here, and the savings
will be a distinct asset to the clothing budget.

EXETER HANDKERCHIEF CO.
REMNANT & DRAPERY STORE

Lincoln Street
Tel. #603-778-8564
Monday-Friday 9:00-4:30
Thursday till 9:00
Saturday 9:00-12:30

This store offers one of the widest selection of drapery and fabric remnants in New England. The choice is excellent, and if you are decorating or redecorating, shopping here will be most worthwhile.

Franklin   *Hosiery*

HOSIERY MILL STORE
Central Street (Route 11)
Tel. #603-934-5452
Monday-Friday 9:00-5:00
Saturday 9:00-4:00

The Hosiery Mill Store carries an excellent assortment of hosiery including socks, stockings, tights, knee socks, crew socks, and fabric slippers. The selection of sizes and colors is certainly ample.

This is a delightful store to visit, and well worth a stop if you are in the general area.

SPAULDING AND FROST
Main Street (Route #107)
Tel. #603-895-3372
Daily Noon-5:00, Closed Wednesdays

Spaulding and Frost offers a complete line of barrels for just about anything imaginable! When did you last see a rain barrel, for instance? Ice buckets, keg stools, planters, hampers, magazine buckets, and sewing buckets are but a few of the items offered in the basic barrel design. Many items are available finished or unfinished.

First quality, seconds, irregulars, and rejects are offered, prices in a sliding scale.

In addition to the array of barrels, the store is located in an interesting 100 year old building. The firm has been engaged in the barrel business for over 105 years.

An interesting place to visit!

THE MILL STORE
Dorr Woolen Company
Routes 11 and 103
Tel. #603-863-1197
Monday-Saturday 9:00-5:00
BankAmericard and Master Charge

Without a doubt, anyone who sews or enjoys related crafts will find a trip here delightful. Initially, the store is attractively landscaped, spacious, well-planned, and parking is provided; as you enter the store, you immediately sense a warm welcome. The layout is such as to display all items to advantage; a tempting array of fabrics, yarns, and related items are easily available.

All fabrics are loomed by the Dorr Woolen Company and include solids, checks, tweeds, and plaids. Suit, coat, dress, and skirt weight woolens, both bonded and not, are offered, either from the bolt or by the piece.

Color coordinated yarns are available for the knitter who wishes to match a sweater and skirt.

Braiding and hooking woolens are available in a spectacular range of colors and shades. Patterns and supplies, as well as helpful suggestions are also available.

To round out the choices is to be found a wide assortment of blankets. Sizes and colors are here to suit everyone's needs.

All in all, this has to be one of the "very special" factory stores.

Hampton   *Paints and Stains*

FLETCHER'S PAINT WORKS
575 Lafayette Road (U.S. Route 1)
Tel. #603-926-6501
Monday-Thursday 8:30-5:30
Friday till 9:00
Saturday 9:00-5:00
BankAmericard and Master Charge

   See Milford, New Hampshire listing.

Keene   *Clothing, (Men's, Women's,*
*   Children's)*

CHARLESTOWN MILL STORE
120 Main Street
Tel. #603-352-2101

   See Charlestown, New Hampshire listing.

Keene   *Children's Stuffed Toys*

DOUGLAS COMPANY FACTORY STORE
West Street
Tel. #603-352-3414
Monday-Saturday 9:00-5:00

This remains an absolutely delightful store! It is worth a visit not only for the children, but for all the rest of us who are young at heart.

The stuffed toys are of all sizes and description. Some are musical. Each is very special; anyone who is a collector would find many delightful specimens. If you are a loving grandparent or aunt, you'll surely find a special toy here.

It has been customary to decorate the store for Christmas, so if you can be in the area after Thanksgiving and before Christmas, be sure to include a stop.

The store is always tastefully set up, the clerks most helpful, and there is easy and ample parking.

Keene   *Paints and Stains*

FLETCHER'S PAINT WORKS
12 Main Street
Tel. #603-352-6044
Monday-Thursday 8:30-5:30
Friday till 9:00
Saturday 9:00-5:00
BankAmericard and Master Charge

See Milford, New Hampshire listing.

Laconia   *Footwear (Men's, Women's,*
Children's)

LACONIA SHOE FACTORY OUTLET
266 Union Avenue (Business Route #3)
Tel. #603-524-9754
Monday-Saturday 9:00-9:00
Sunday 1:00-5:00
BankAmericard and Master Charge

This very large outlet store has an excellent
assortment of shoes for men, women, and children.
Both dress and casual styles are available in an
ample range of sizes. Sneakers are also available
here.

A unique factor here is a small trade-in allowance
on used shoes. This practice was noted during a
recent visit; however, remember that such a feature
could change and/or be discontinued.

Lots of choices should provide something for
almost everyone.

Laconia   *Paints and Stains*

FLETCHER'S PAINT WORKS
1315 Union Avenue
Tel. #603-524-3270
Monday-Thursday 8:30-5:30
Friday till 9:00
Saturday 9:00-5:00
BankAmericard and Master Charge

See Milford, New Hampshire listing.

Laconia (Lakeport)   *Clothing*

SWEATERVILLE, U.S.A.
Bayside Ct.
Tel. #603-524-4660
Monday-Saturday 9:00-5:30
Thursday and Friday till 9:00
Sunday 12:00-6:00

See Wolfeboro, New Hampshire listing.

Lebanon   *Paints and Stains*

FLETCHER'S PAINT WORKS
2 Campbell Street
Tel. #603-448-4006
Monday-Thursday 8:30-5:30
Friday till 9:00
Saturday 9:00-5:00
BankAmericard and Master Charge

See Milford, New Hampshire listing.

Lisbon   *Furniture*

SUGAR HILL SHOWROOM
Main Street
Tel. #603-838-6677
Monday-Saturday 9:30-5:30
Sunday afternoons seasonal

The Sugar Hill Showroom offers an excellent selection of "furniture seconds to take home." A variety of bedroom, dining room, living room and occasional pieces are offered and are designed to reflect the New England style. In addition, their Country Bargain Gift Shop offers an excellent selection of gifts and household accessories.

Certainly an interesting place to visit.

Littleton   *Paints and Stains*

FLETCHER'S PAINT WORKS
Main Street
Tel. #603-444-5721
Monday-Thursday 8:30-5:30
Friday till 9:00
Saturday 9:00-5:00
BankAmericard and Master Charge

See Milford, New Hampshire listing.

SARANAC GLOVE COMPANY
6-8 Main Street
Tel. #603-444-2210
Monday-Saturday 8:30-6:00
Friday till 9:00
Sundays - Seasonal

An interesting place to visit, the Saranac Glove Company store offers an unbelievable assortment of deerskin gloves suitable for practically every situation. Gloves and mittens for the entire family are available and include such categories as dress, casual, work, skiing, snowmobile, hunting, golf, and gardening. In addition, the Glen of Michigan line of ladies sportswear will be found; also mocassins, handbags, and leather accessories are available.

You can see the various steps taking place in the factory. Certainly the ample selection, the helpful sales personnel, and the interesting factory are all aspects of this factory store which make a trip here a special experience.

Manchester   *Shoes (Women's)*

DORSON-FLEISHER INC.
South Willow Street (Route 28)
Tel. #603-627-7891
Thursday 10:00-9:00
Friday and Saturday 10:00-5:00

A nice assortment of women's shoes will be found
at Dorson-Fleisher. The range of styles, colors,
materials, and sizes makes a trip here usually
successful.

Helpful sales personnel, the ease of parking, and
the selection combine to make a trip here a good
experience.

Manchester   *Clothing (Men's, Women's*
Children's) Yarns

PANDORA FACTORY STORE
Dow and Canal Streets
Tel. #603-668-4802
Monday-Saturday 9:30-5:30
Monday, Thursday, Friday till 9:00
Sunday 9:30-5:00
More extensive hours in summer
BankAmericard and Master Charge

This continues to be one of the outstanding
factory stores. It is large, well laid out, and staffed
by helpful sales personnel. Certainly a seasonal
shopping expedition here would help any family's
clothing budget.

The stock of women's, men's, and children's
sweaters is sure to provide the widest choices in
colors, styles, and sizes. Women's slacks, skirts,
and sweaters are available in color coordinated sets.
For men, tailored shirts, pants, golf and ski wear,
and for youngsters, play and school clothes in
machine washable fabrics are available.

In addition, fabrics, yarn for knitting, and trims,
buttons, and zippers are available, to coordinate
with the Pandora, Candia, and Brookshire lines.

Ample parking and the maintenance of a mailing
list are added features of an already super factory
store!

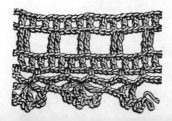

Manchester   *Shoes (Family)*

THOM McAN FACTORY OUTLET
345 Main Street
Tel. #603-623-8024
Monday-Saturday 9:00-5:00
Thursday till 9:00

See Dover New Hampshire listing.

Manchester   *Fabrics*

WAUMBEC MILL FABRIC STORE
Amoskeag Mill Yard
Stark Street
Tel. #603-625-8593
Monday-Saturday 8:30-5:00
BankAmericard and Master Charge

An excellent assortment of fabrics will be found
here, including polyester double knits, 100% wool,
wool blends and woven dresswear fabric. In
addition, drapery and curtain materials are
available.

The large selection and the very helpful sales
personnel make a trip here rewarding.

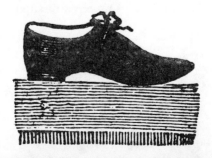

Meredith   *Dolls (Display and Decoration)*

ANNALEE'S WORKSHOP
Off Route #3
Tel. #603-279-6543
Sunday-Saturday 9:00-5:00
Easter to Christmas only

Annalee's Workshop is an enchanting shop to visit. The assortment of holiday and special occasion dolls are elfin in character, and sure to delight any visitor to the Workshop. Although only a few items are offered at any saving over the normal retail price, the shop is well worth a visit, for the atmosphere is just delightful.

One annual sale is held the weekend after New Year's and is well attended!

Merrimack   *Furniture*

PILGRIM VILLAGE
FURNITURE SHOWROOM
Route #3
Tel. #603-424-5544, 603-424-2181
Monday-Thursday 8:30-5:30
Friday and Saturday 8:30-5:30
Sunday 12:00-5:00

This Showroom features the pine furniture made
by the Pilgrim Pine Factory. The style is Early
American, and the reproductions are authentic in
design. The selection is exceptional and you should
be able to find any piece you need for your home.

Grandfather and grandmother clocks, Tiffany
type glass fixtures, rugs, lamps, and accessories are
also available.

In addition, a factory tour is available, to make
your stop interesting, as well as beneficial to the
budget.

FLETCHER'S PAINT WORKS
Route 101
Tel. #603-673-2300
Monday-Thursday 8:30-5:30
Friday till 9:00
Saturday 9:00-5:00
BankAmericard and Master Charge

BRANCH STORES:
1315 Union Avenue
Laconia, New Hampshire
Tel. #603-524-3270
Monday-Thursday 8:30-5:30
Friday till 9:00
Saturday 9:00-5:30
Saturday 9:00-5:00
BankAmericard and Master Charge

2 Campbell Street
Lebanon, New Hampshire
Tel. #603-448-4006
Monday-Thursday 8:30-5:30
Friday till 9:00
Saturday 9:00-5:00
BankAmericard and Master Charge

Milford

76 North Main Street
Concord, New Hampshire
Tel. #603-225-2198
Monday-Thursday 8:30-5:30
Friday till 9:00
Saturday 9:00-5:00
BankAmericard and Master Charge

Main Street
Littleton, New Hampshire
Tel. #603-444-5721
Monday-Thursday 8:30-5:30
Friday till 9:00
Saturday 9:00-5:00
BankAmericard and Master Charge

12 Main Street
Keene, New Hampshire
Tel. #603-352-6044
Monday-Thursday 8:30-5:30
Friday till 9:00
Saturday 9:00-5:00
BankAmericard and Master Charge

575 Lafayette Road (U.S. Route 1)
Hampton, New Hampshire
Tel. #603-926-6501
Monday-Thursday 8:30-5:30
Friday till 9:00
Saturday 9:00-5:00
BankAmericard and Master Charge

Central Street
Woodsville, New Hampshire
Tel. #603-747-3743
Monday-Thursday 8:30-5:30
Friday till 9:00
Saturday 9:00-5:00
BankAmericard and Master Charge

Fletcher's extensive line of paints and stains may be found either at the factory store itself, or at any of the branch stores. The paints are available in either oil base or acrylic latex in authentic colonial colors; the solid color stains are available in either latex or oil; the semi-transparent stains are available in oil base only.

The choice of colors is excellent, and particularly suited to New England tradition. The paints are designed for New England weather, so should protect the wood from New England's tempermental climate.

Nashua   *Coats (Men's, Women's)*

ANTHONY ROBERTS, INC.
Route 3A
210 Daniel Webster Highway
Tel. #603-888-0722

See Milford, Massachusetts listing.

Nashua   *Shoes (Family)*

THOM McAN FACTORY OUTLET
9 Spruce Street
Tel. #603-889-6108
Monday-Saturday 9:00-5:00
Thursday till 9:00

See Dover, New Hampshire listing.

Newport   *Jewelry (Costume)*

WIPCO JEWELRY COMPANY
Route 11
Tel. #603-863-1351
April-December
Monday-Friday 9:00-5:00
Saturday 9:00-4:00
Check by phone during other months, and for
extended hours during December.

The extensive selection of costume jewelry is
large enough to tempt most of us who wear costume
jewelry. There is also a tremendous supply of gift
items and a catalog store from which selections may
be made, but it is the jewelry which warrants
Wipco's inclusion in this Guide.

Ample parking is provided, and a trip here is
easily combined with one to Manchester,
Charlestown, or Guild, making the trip worthwhile.

New Ipswich *Clothing (Women's)*

UPS 'N' DOWNS MILL OUTLET
King Street
Tel. # - None
Sunday-Saturday 9:00-5:00
Thursday-Sunday till 9:00

This outlet store offers primarily body shirts (turtleneck style), stockings, and socks in a nice variety of colors and sizes. Some children's clothing such as slacks, and some ladies' slacks are to be found, as is a sprinkling of other clothing items.

Newmarket *Furniture*

DRAKE SMITH & CO. FACTORY OUTLET
Main Street (Route #108)
Tel. #603-659-5443
Monday-Saturday 9:00-5:30
Friday till 8:30
Sunday 1:00-5:30
BankAmericard and Master Charge

Drake Smith offers truly lovely native pine colonial furniture manufactured both in Newmarket and Bristol, Vermont. Bedroom, living room, and dining room furniture pieces are attractively displayed in the very large showroom located in the big Brick Mill. It would seem difficult not to find just the right piece here, if your taste is the colonial style.

This store is a delightful place in which to shop.

North Conway   *Cookware, Giftware*

DANSK FACTORY OUTLET
Route 16
Tel. #603-356-3493
10:00-5:30 7 days a week

See Kittery, Maine listing.

North Conway   *Clothing (Men's, Women's)*

KITTERY MILLS OF NORTH CONWAY
North Conway
Tel. #603-356-5438
Sunday-Saturday 10:00-6:00
Friday and Saturday till 9:00

See Kittery, Maine listing.

ARTISAN OUTLET
Mirona Road
Tel. #603-436-0022
Monday-Friday 10:00-9:00
Saturday 10:00-6:00
Sunday 1:00-6:00

BRANCH STORES:
Wells Corner (Rte. 1)
Wells, Maine
Tel. #207-646-2750
Open 7 days

Midtown Mall
Sanford, Maine
Tel. #207-324-7558
Monday-Saturday only

POORE SIMON'S FOR MEN
DeMoulas Shopping Plaza
Route 1
Seabrook, New Hampshire
Tel. #603-474-9426
Open 7 days

The Artisan Outlet offers excellent opportunities to save on both women's and men's clothing. Sweaters, shirts, skirts, slacks, dresses, and sportswear are on the racks in a wide variety of styles and colors, while in the men's department will be found a fine selection of shirts, trousers, and sweaters. **Poore Simon's** is exclusively for men, so a much larger selection is there.

Shoes are found in the Portsmouth store, and again, a good selection of sizes and styles is available.

There is ample parking, and the stores are staffed by courteous sales people.

SWEATERVILLE, U.S.A.
Maplewood Avenue
Rte. 1 By-Pass
Tel. #603-436-5521
Monday-Friday 9:30-9:30
Saturday 10:00-5:30
Sunday 12:00-6:00

See Wolfeboro, New Hampshire listing.

WEST RINDGE BASKETS, INC.
Off Route #202 (West Rindge)
Tel. #603-899-2231
Monday-Thursday 7:30-5:30

If you are looking for an authentic, made in New England ash basket, the West Rindge Baskets shop is the place to go. A variety of basket styles will be found here, some of which are considered seconds, and offered at a saving.

You can watch the baskets being made, an interesting craft which has changed very little over the years.

This is really a delightful shop to visit; if you cannot visit, they do have a mail order business.

Seabrook   *Clothing, Shoes*

POORE SIMON'S FOR MEN
DeMoulas Shopping Plaza
Route 1
Tel. #603-474-9426
Open 7 days

See Portsmouth, New Hampshire listing - Artisan
Outlet.

Suncook   *Furniture*

THE MILL STORE, INC.
Main Street
Tel. #603-485-5100
Wednesday and Thursday 8:30-5:30
Friday 8:30-8:00
Saturday 9:00-5:00
Sunday 1:00-5:00
BankAmericard and Master Charge

The Mill Store, Inc. offers an excellent selection of
colonial furniture. First quality, damaged, and
irregular items are offered, with savings relative to
the category.

If you are looking for furniture which says New
England, this is a good place to shop.

HOMESTEAD WOOLEN MILL STORE
Winchester Street
Tel. #603-352-2023
Daily 9:00-5:00

A nice assortment of both all wool and wool blend fabrics is to be found here. The mill is located across the street, so the selection is updated regularly. Solid colors, plaids, and patterns are available.

Both the home sewer and the rug braider will find the selection to be good.

Adequate parking is available.

Wilton   *Woodenware*

FRYE'S FIRKIN WORKS
Off Route #31
Tel. #603-654-4811
Daily 10:00-5:00
(Summer Season)

The handcrafted woodenware items offered at
Frye's are truly "authentic survivors of 19th
century craftsmanship and technology" for the
wooden containers and Shaker reproduction items
are made in the mill which has been in existence
since 1861.

The round colonial boxes and the oval Shaker
boxes are most attractive and are accurate
reproductions. Some wooden toys, two sizes of
wooden dye dippers, and wooden measures are also
to be found.

If you are traveling in southern New Hampshire,
this intriguing mill is well worth visiting. The
atmosphere has that "something special," and a
box, toy, or other wooden items from here will be a
treasured reminder of New England.

The Shop area is not heated; hence once the cold
weather sets in, it is closed.

Wolfeboro   *Clothing*

SWEATERVILLE, U.S.A.
Main Street
Tel. #603-569-3400
Monday-Saturday 9:00-5:30

BRANCH STORES:
Bayside Ct.
Laconia, N.H. (Lakeport)
Tel. #603-524-4660
Monday-Saturday 9:00-5:30
Thursday and Friday till 9:00
Sunday 12:00-6:00

Maplewood Avenue
Rte. 1 By-Pass
Portsmouth, N.H.
Tel. #603-436-5521
Monday-Friday 9:30-9:30
Saturday 10:00-5:30
Sunday 12:00-5:00

The advertisements for Sweaterville, U.S.A. say "select from 20,000 sweaters;" with this selection, how could you miss? In addition, sports apparel including ski wear, parkas, and snowmobile wear, as well as dresses, suits, and jackets are all to be found.

The store certainly offers a good deal of merchandise for the whole family. The selection is really ample, and the savings are most helpful.

FLETCHER'S PAINT WORKS
Central Street
Tel. #603-747-3743
Monday-Thursday 8:30-5:30
Friday till 9:00
Saturday 9:00-5:00
BankAmericard and Master Charge

See Milford, New Hampshire listing.

COASTAL FASHIONS OUTLET
Bangor Shopping Center
Tel. #207-942-1664
Monday-Saturday 9:30-10:00
Sunday 10:00-6:00
BankAmericard and Master Charge

See Ellsworth, Maine listing.

DALY BROTH. BEDDING COMPANY
Five Points
Tel. #207-282-9583
Monday-Friday 9:00-5:00
Friday till 8:00
Saturday 9:00-12:00

The Daly Brothers store offers Maiden Maine
mattresses in their full range of sizes and styles.

EMPLE KNITTING MILLS
Bar Harbor Road
Tel. #207-989-4780
Monday-Saturday 7:30-4:30

The Emple store offers an outstanding
assortment of sweaters for men and women. Sizes
go up to extra large, and the variety of styles and
colors practically insures something for everyone.
In addition, famous brands of knits for women will
be found here, offering dresses, suits, slacks, and
blouses. The choice of colors and styles is excellent.

The store is air conditioned for summer shoppers.
It really is a delightful, financially rewarding trip,
which should help stretch your clothing budget.

Ellsworth   *Fabrics,*
                                           Blankets

CASCADE FABRICS
125 High Street (Routes 1 and 3)
Tel. #207-667-5894
Monday-Saturday 9:00-5:00
Summer Hours
Open evenings and Sunday 1:00-5:00

See Oakland, Maine listing.

COASTAL FASHIONS OUTLET
Maine Coast Mall
Tel. 207-667-5097
Monday-Saturday 9:00-9:00
Sunday 9:00-5:00
BankAmericard and Master Charge

BRANCH STORE:
Bangor Shopping Center
Bangor, Maine
Tel. #207-942-1664
Monday-Saturday 9:30-10:00
Sunday 10:00-6:00
BankAmericard and Master Charge

A very good assortment of women's sportswear is
to be found at the Coastal Fashions store. Skirts,
shirts, slacks, jackets, and tops in a wide
assortment of colors, styles, and sizes are available.

Since the stores are located in shopping malls,
they are easy to locate, and give the shopper the opportunity to do a variety of shopping in one trip.

FORMFIT ROGERS OUTLET STORE
Maine Coast Mall (Rte. 1 & 3)
Tel. #207-667-9267
Monday-Saturday 9:00-9:00
Sunday 10:00-5:00 (In summer)

The Formfit Rogers Store offers an excellent assortment of lingerie, including bras, girdles, bikini panties, briefs, slips, robes, nightgowns, and pajamas. Sizes and styles are in ample variety, and both first quality and irregular items will be found.

The location in the shopping mall with its adjacent factory stores as well as a wide variety of regular stores, makes this an easy, desirable place to shop.

THE FREEPORT COMPANY OUTLET
21 Mill Street
Tel. #207-865-6326
Monday-Friday 9:00-3:00

This small factory is producing unique molded urethane placques. The process is clearly explained, and the placques while giving the appearance of a "picture" within a frame, are actually one piece. They are attractively executed and are available in a variety of designs.

GUILFORD MILL STORE
Main Street
Tel. #207-876-3331
Monday-Saturday 8:00-5:00
Sunday 12:00-5:00
BankAmericard

Wool blends and polyesters are featured at the
Guilford Mill Store. Other fabrics are available;
they are, however, usually priced at regular retail.

The selection is ample, and certainly, if you are a
sewer and you are in the area, a trip here should be
worthwhile.

BARTLETT YARNS, INC.
South Road
Tel. #207-683-2251
Monday-Friday 9:00-4:00

For anyone interested in yarns for various hand crafts, a visit here is a delightful experience! Pure wool yarns are available for knitters, spinners, weavers, and craftsmen who prefer the sturdiness, strength, and springy resiliency of wool. A variety of colors and types is available; in addition, accessories such as looms have been stocked. Custom spinning of your own fleece can also be done.

The mill is open to visitors, and is very interesting. Historically, the mills date back to 1821. If you are in the area, a visit here will be rewarding, regardless of whether you are a crafts person or not.

DANSK FACTORY OUTLET
Route 1, Kittery Mall
Tel. #207-439-0484
Sunday-Saturday 9:00-6:00
Friday till 9:00
Longer hours at seasonal times

BRANCH STORE:
Route 16
North Conway, New Hampshire
Tel. #603-356-3493
10:00-5:30 7 days

The Dansk Factory Outlet store offers an
extensive array of the various Dansk kitchen and
cookware items, as well as of their giftware. The
large selection makes shopping here a delightful
experience, with everything from candleholders to
dishes on display.

The easy accessibility, the large parking area, the
helpful sales personnel, and the excellent selection
are all factors which combine to make this a
pleasant shopping trip.

KITTERY MILLS, INC.
Route 1, Kittery Mall
Tel. #207-439-4258
Sunday-Saturday 10:00-5:30
Friday till 8:00

BRANCH STORES:
Kittery Mills of Ogunquit
Beach Street
Ogunquit, Maine
Tel. # - None listed
Summer only

Kittery Mills of Hyannis (Ladies only)
585 Main Street
Hyannis, Massachusetts
Tel. #617-775-6122
Sunday-Saturday 10:00-5:30
Friday till 8:00

Kittery Mills of North Conway
North Conway, New Hampshire
Tel. #603-356-5438
Sunday-Saturday 10:00-6:00
Friday and Saturday till 9:00

The Kittery Mills store offers an excellent
assortment of leading brands of men's shirts,
sportswear for men and women, sweaters, robes,
and ties for men. Both irregulars and first quality
closeouts are to be found here. The wide range of
styles, colors, and sizes makes for good shopping.

BATES MILL STORE
Canal and Chestnut Street
Tel. #207-784-7311
Monday-Friday 8:00-5:00
Saturday 9:00-1:00
BankAmericare and Master Charge

Bates Mill Store offers a wide selection of Bates
Bedspreads and Table fashions, as well as mattress
pads, blankets, towels, and sheets. The items are
close-out styles and irregulars. A broad choice of
styles, colors, and sizes is available.

Ample parking is available.

The Bates mill itself is the largest jacquard woven
bedspread plant in the world, and is also the most
integrated facility of its kind in the world, as it
carries out all the stages in bedspread production.

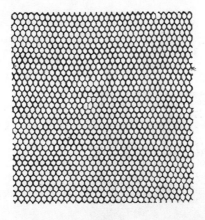

Oakland   *Fabrics,*
                                                 Blankets

THE MILL STORE
Cascade Woolen Mill
Route 137
Tel. #207-465-2511
Monday-Saturday 8:30-4:30

BRANCH STORE:
CASCADE FABRICS
125 High Street (Routes 1 and 3)
Ellsworth
Tel. #207-667-5894
Monday-Saturday 9:00-5:00
Summer Hours -
Open evenings and Sunday 1:00-5:00

Featured is an outstanding assortment of over
200 styles and colors of all wool fabrics. If you are a
sewer, the range of patterns and colors should
provide ample inspiration for skirts, suits, jackets,
and slacks.

In addition, attractive blankets are available.

Easy parking and the excellent selection combine
to make a visit here worthwhile.

Ogunquit   *Clothing (Men's, Women's)*

KITTERY MILLS OF OGUNQUIT
Beach Street
Tel. # - None listed
Summer only

See Kittery, Maine listing.

Oxford Village   *Fabrics*

OXFORD MILL-END STORE
Robinson Mfg. Co.
King Street
Tel. #207-539-4451
Monday-Saturday 9:00-5:00

This delightful shop offers a good assortment of yard goods, remnants, yarn, and rug material. In fact, of all the stores offering woolen remnants for rug braiding, the Mill-End Store has been one of the most reasonable.

Their woolen yard goods are especially suited for coats, skirts, slacks, and suits.

This is a particularly pleasant store in which to shop; a trip here can be combined with one to Oxford Yankee Workshop, making a shopping trip more practical.

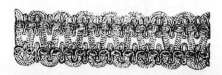

OXFORD YANKEE WORKSHOP
Route 26
Tel. #207-743-7421
Monday-Saturday 9:00-6:00
BankAmericard and Master Charge

The Oxford Yankee Workshop is a very large shop stocking wooden furniture and gift items, predominantly traditional in style. Both factory seconds and first quality merchandise are available here.

A marvelous bin containing a large variety of wood turnings is available for hobbyists. If you have any need for these small wooden items, this is certainly an excellent source.

The vast amount of items from which to choose, the delightful shop, and the ease of parking are all factors which make it an interesting shop to visit. By planning to include the Mill End Store, a trip to Oxford can do dual duty.

FRENCH SHRINER OUTLET
1108 Forest Avenue
Tel. #207-797-4689
Monday-Saturday 9:30-6:00
Thursday till 9:00
BankAmericard and Master Charge

An excellent selection of both men's and women's shoes is available here. Dress, casual, and sport styles are to be found; the shoes may be cancellations, discontinued styles, or may have slight imperfections.

To be able to purchase shoes of this quality at a large savings should be most helpful to anyone's budget.

PORTLAND STOVE FOUNDRY
57 Kennebec Street
Tel. #207-773-0256
Monday-Saturday 9:00-4:00

With the current upswing of interest in wood burning stoves, a visit to the Portland Stove Foundry should be interesting. They have available seven different models of the Franklin Stove alone, as well as a good selection of wood cook stoves, box stoves, parlor stoves, and pot belly stoves.

If you wish to supplement your present heating system, a trip here will provide you with alternatives. Be sure you thoroughly understand the ramifications of using such stoves; this store is the place to ask your questions.

W. SPENCER, INC.
446 Fore Street
Tel. #207-773-0552
Monday-Friday 8:30-4:00

The W. Spencer company offers delightful and educational tours of their candle factory. Its location in the historic Old Port Exchange area of Portland, gives the visitor a chance to see some of the Georgian and Greek Revival architecture of the once bustling port area.

In addition to watching the working craftsmen pouring and decorating the candles, visitors also have the opportunity to dip a candle.

A trip to Spencer's opens the door to an interesting craft. For children, as well as adults, it provides an interesting change from the normal shopping venture.

VAN BAALEN PACIFIC OUTLET STORE
Route 1
Tel. #207-596-6646
Monday-Friday 9:00-5:00
Saturday 9:00-12:00

An excellent selection of men's clothing will be
found here. Sportswear including sport shirts,
shorts, and slacks, as well as an impressive array of
robes, are available in a good choice of sizes and
colors, In addition, some lingerie for women is
available; also yard goods are available.

The nice selection, the helpful sales personnel,
and the location on the scenic coast of Maine are all
factors which combine to make this a delightful trip.

Sanford   *Clothing, Shoes*

ARTISAN OUTLET
Midtown Mall
Tel. #207-324-7558
Monday-Saturday only

See Portsmouth, New Hampshire listing.

SEAMLOC
River Street
Tel. #207-324-2233
Monday-Friday 10:00-5:00
Saturday 10:00-1:00
BankAmericard and Master Charge

Seamloc is a contract manufacturer of wool and synthetic fiber carpets. Short rolls and overruns of their products are available in their mill store. A wide selection is available, with an excellent choice of colors, textures, weaves, and patterns. It is sponge rubber backed, and because it is fully woven rather than tufted, it does not require binding on the edges.

Runners, scatter rugs, and bundles of squares which may be laid in a design of your own are also available here.

Certainly an excellent stop if you are seeking fine quality carpeting.

Springvale   *Clothing (Women's)*

SPRINGVALE SPORTSWEAR INC.
Mill Street
Tel. #207-324-3535
Tuesday-Friday 10:00-5:00
Saturday 10:00-3:00

A nice assortment of women's sportswear,
including slacks, tops, shorts, and bathing suits is
to be found here. Particularly a plus factor is the
nice selection of the larger sizes.

Some fabrics and trims are also available.

The helpful sales personnel, the nice assortment
of sportswear in larger sizes, and the ample parking
are all factors which help to make a trip here
successful.

Wells   *Clothing, Shoes*

ARTISAN OUTLET
Wells Corner (Route 1)
Tel. #207-646-2750
Open 7 days

See Portsmouth, New Hampshire listing.

Towle silver - Newburyport, Mass.